"Life after divorce is not only about trying to redefine the new normal but also about trying to redefine a new future in light of all the fears and consequences of the past. This book is a compass for anyone trying to navigate the uncharted waters of life after divorce."

Chris Brown, Teaching Pastor
North Coast Church

"David and Lisa Frisbie share wise and timely insights for divorced persons who are considering entering into a new marriage relationship. They draw from their two decades of experience ministering to persons who are bravely attempting to survive and thrive after a divorce."

Jerry Porter, General Superintendent
Church of the Nazarene

"I highly recommend this new resource for divorced adults!"

H. Wayne Hose, Executive Vice President
Believe & Receive New Life Ministries

"David and Lisa are among the very few Christian voices that speak practical, biblical truth to people who have lived through the pain and change of divorce. Their words bring hope, help, and healing while addressing the challenges faced by people asking tough questions about remarriage."

Brett Rickey, Senior Pastor
Highland Park Church of the Nazarene, Lakeland, Florida

DATING *after* DIVORCE

preparing for a new relationship

DAVID&LISA FRISBIE

BEACON HILL PRESS
OF KANSAS CITY

Copyright 2012
by David and Lisa Frisbie and Beacon Hill Press of Kansas City

ISBN 978-0-8341-2882-8

Printed in the
United States of America

Cover Design: J.R. Caines
Inside Design: Sharon Page

All Scripture quotations are from the *New King James Version* (NKJV).
Copyright © 1979, 1980, 1982 Thomas Nelson, Inc.

Library of Congress Cataloging-in-Publication Data

Frisbie, David, 1955-
   Dating after divorce : preparing for a new relationship / David Frisbie and
Lisa Frisbie.
      p. cm.
   Includes bibliographical references (p.   ).
   ISBN 978-0-8341-2882-8 (pbk.)
   1. Divorced people—Religious life. 2. Divorce—Religious aspects—
Christianity. 3. Man-woman relationships—Religious aspects—
Christianity. 4. Dating (Social customs)—Religious aspects—
Christianity. I. Frisbie, Lisa, 1956- II. Title.
   BV4596.D58F745 2012
   248.8'46—dc23
                                                                    2012011675

10 9 8 7 6 5 4 3 2 1

CONTENTS

Dedication and Acknowledgments   7

After Divorce—

   1. Are You Ready for a New Relationship?   11

   2. Are You Financially Prepared?   22

   3. Are You Emotionally Prepared?   49

   4. Are You Spiritually Prepared?   76

   5. Are You Physically Prepared?   101

   6. Is Your Family Prepared?   127

   7. Divorce Roundtable: A Free-flowing Conversation
      with Divorced Men and Women   157

Recommended Reading   183

About the Authors   185

DEDICATION AND ACKNOWLEDGMENTS

This book is dedicated to my students both past and present. All of you have been a joy to learn with and a blessing to know. All of you have contributed a wealth of wisdom to the growing body of relevant and useful knowledge in family studies and gerontology. Your life experiences, your discernment, your ability to sort out the practical from the merely academic—each one of you brings a lot to the classroom. I enjoy learning with you and from you.

For several decades now, Lisa and I have held the unsolicited title of "America's Remarriage Experts." This label was originally stuck on us by a daily newspaper in the Midwest. At the time we had no idea how adhesive that label would prove to be. Even many years later, when an editor at Group Publishing called to invite us to contribute a chapter on remarriage to an anthology project, we asked him why he called us out of so many available authors and contributors.

His answer? "Well, after all, you're the experts!"

It's somewhat intimidating to be the experts in any field, but perhaps that's the danger of devoting two decades of our adult lives to studying and learning about the post-divorce family. That landscape—divorced adults, single parents, remarried couples, step-families, blended families—is where we've done our intellectual hiking and backpacking for more than twenty years now. So yes, we do know the terrain of the world of a divorced adult, remarried or not. It's where we have lived and worked and studied and learned since the late 1980s.

We would argue that an adult who is coping with a divorce, learning how to raise kids alone, considering or entering into remarriage, or struggling to blend a family is the true expert.

People facing these kinds of challenges want to know what works. *Will it work for me?* So by trial and error—and life brings plenty of both—practical knowledge advances, and useful wisdom is formed.

This brings us back to where we started: my students. I am thinking of you right now as I write this dedication. I am visualizing our classrooms in the old campus and also in the new campus. I am remembering your projects and presentations and findings. I am recalling the lively discussions we have shared together, especially the case studies.

I am also remembering your graduations—watching and listening—as your children, your parents, your spouses, and your friends cheered and yelled and clapped and whistled and celebrated as you were awarded your degrees. Lisa and I were there; she was dressed beautifully and sitting in the bleachers, and I was robed and hooded and draped and walking with the faculty. Both of us were cheering along with your families and friends.

I was proud of you on that day—and all the days that led up to it—proud of you for working hard, balancing competing and conflicting priorities, moving forward steadily despite setbacks and challenges—poverty, job losses, and sometimes homelessness.

You didn't quit or give up. You wouldn't settle for less. You studied, learned, did your reading, and did your writing. You gave wonderful presentations of your findings, and you contributed to discussions with counselors and peers and educators.

For those of you who have not yet graduated: your day is coming.

For all of you who have graced my classrooms on the two campuses, even for those of you who suffered when I was pressed into duty to teach religion, this book is dedicated to you with my profound gratitude.

I say what I mean, and I mean what I say.

It is a blessing and a joy to learn with you.

one

ARE YOU READY FOR A NEW RELATIONSHIP?

After more than two decades of studying the post-divorce family, we are still learning new things. Our work as family counselors brings us a constant stream of adults who are divorced, plus adults who experienced divorce as children when they were growing up. We are constantly learning about divorce and its effects on family life, emotional development, spiritual formation, and more.

There is much more we still need to learn, but here is what we can tell you with absolute certainty: some of the most mature, wisest, most spiritually advanced people we know have experienced the end of a marriage. They are divorced, and they are also spiritual, mature, wise, and well-balanced.

This is an accurate description of the findings from our work with children, adolescents, university students, adults, and seniors in and out of all types of family environments and family situations.

Some of the most godly, most spiritually mature pastors and leaders we have encountered are divorced, and some of them have since remarried. Some of the most Spirit-filled women we've met—and we've met many—have experienced divorce during their adult lifetimes. Day in and day out, some of the people who most impress us with their emotional stability, spiritual perspective, knowledge of God's Word, and service to God's kingdom are people who have been through the pain of a divorce during their adult lives. Divorce happened to them, yet they found a way to move forward to newfound depth and clarity in their personal lives and in their walks with God.

Are we suggesting that in order to grow and become mature, everyone should run out and get divorced? God forbid.

Every divorce is a tragedy. Even when someone's life improves as a result of a divorce—and candidly this is sometimes the case—divorce is still a tragedy. Divorce means a promise was made but broken. Divorce means a relationship was begun but a commitment was not kept. Divorce brings loss and pain and hardship and difficulty, and it's a gift that keeps on giving in those categories.

Yet somehow divorce also produces an environment that causes people to awaken more fully to the questions of sincere faith, to the journey of seeking after God, to the duties we all have to each other as we share this small planet. For whatever reason, even otherwise godly and mature adults can sometimes end up "going deeper" after they experience the trauma and heartache of divorce.

Once again, please understand what we are *not* saying. We are not recommending divorce. We work against it with all our strength, day after day. We often watch God repair completely impossible relationships—people and marriages that seem broken beyond all hope of redemption. In our daily work as marriage therapists, family counselors, and pastoral ministers, we have watched God do amazing things in the midst of impossible pain.

God hates divorce, and so do we.

But God loves people who have experienced divorce, and so do we. We get to work with those people day after day in our office or our classrooms or at church. We get to learn with and learn from men and women who are going through the end of a marriage and coming out the other side wiser, more open to change, and realizing that growth brought on by that pain can be good.

We are incredibly grateful to the many divorced men and women who have shared their journeys with us, telling us the stories of their lives in the counseling office or around the table at a coffee shop. We have learned a lot, and we are still learning. Our work with divorced adults is constant and ongoing.

Within the context of this particular book we raise the question: how would a divorced person know if he or she were ready for a new relationship? What are the markers of emotional health, spiritual health, and other types of health that would let the person know that it's okay to move forward and be open to new beginnings?

That specific focus is at the core of this book. It is the main question we address, even though we look at it five different ways in five main chapters and also from many different perspectives and many different sources.

WHAT THIS BOOK IS NOT

This book is not a theology of marriage or a theology of divorce. There are some wonderful books you might consult if you love exploring theology; we'll list them among the recommended reading at the back of the book. If you are hoping for a college-level or graduate-level textbook on the theology of marriage and divorce, this won't be the book for you.

About theology, let us simply say that God designed marriage to be a lifelong commitment between two persons—one man and one woman. Both the Old Testament and the New Testament make it clear that a husband and wife belong to each other for as long as they both live. It is not until after death that the surviving spouse is free of his or her marriage and the term of the marriage has reached its conclusion. Marriage, as God designed it and intended it, lasts a lifetime. He never had anything else in mind.

Meanwhile, as human beings began living on earth and trying to fulfill God's good purposes, marriages somehow found ways to end. Way back in the earliest days of biblical history, adults were badgering the prophets to grant them a few loopholes in case marriage didn't work out. People wanted to dispose of a marriage but still be right in the sight of God. You might call this trying to have it both ways.

Jesus called it something else. He called it being stubborn and difficult to teach. As Jesus is teaching and preaching, the religious leaders of the day—in this case some Pharisees—raise the question of divorce with Him. Jesus responds with a strong defense of marriage, explaining that God always intended marriage to last a lifetime.

"Yes," the Pharisees object, "but Moses granted us permission to get a divorce." Here the devout religious leaders are accurate in their reading of Scripture. But what they are really doing in this discussion is trying to find out whether Jesus agrees or disagrees with Moses. Here's a hint: anyone who wishes to be orthodox in his or her faith had better agree with Moses.

Jesus firmly and wisely brings them back to the main issue.

"Moses gave you permission to divorce only because you are stubborn and hard to teach," Jesus explains. "But it was not like that at the time of creation." Jesus explains that God always intended for marriage to last a lifetime. Just in case there is any doubt, Jesus goes on to affirm that if a man divorces his wife for any reason other than her unfaithfulness, he commits adultery if he then goes out and marries someone else. (See Matthew 19:1-11 and Mark 10:1-12.)

That being said, there is no need for us to invent a theology of marriage or divorce. We can tell what God's plan is, what His purposes are, and how He wants us to live. We have access to Scripture, and within its pages we find what Jesus had to say on the record regarding ending a marriage or starting over.

The primary issue we address in this book is that of *starting over*. How will you know when or if it is time to start over? When would it be wise to avoid any possible new relationships, and when might it be okay to consider exploring a friendship or a romance with someone?

- How much time needs to pass after a marriage ends?
- How much healing needs to be done in yourself or others?
- How much maturity needs to be achieved in you—and your potential new life partner?
- Do you need to be perfect, whole, and well balanced before you begin thinking about dating again, finding someone else, or getting remarried?

Here's another disclaimer before you proceed through this book: we are not going to recommend that you date or remarry; we are not going to recommend that you remain single for life; and we are not going to take a position on those issues. Those are decisions you will need to make, because, after all, it's your life. You are the one who must make those decision, and you are the one who will be affected by the decisions you make.

WHAT THIS BOOK IS

We've met hundreds of divorced adults who decided that the wisest and best thing for them would be to remain single. So they did, and they went on to become whole, mature, wise, well-balanced single adults who make important contributions to the Kingdom and society every day.

Where is it written that a person must be married in order to be wise? Where is it written that a person must be married to serve the Lord?

Our little planet needs more single-adult Christians to serve as role models. Our world needs to see that it is more than okay to be single—single people serve, help, achieve, contribute, go on to reach maturity, and honor God with their lives. Singles do all these things. Single men and women are not defective or deficient or "less than" anyone else.

What this book *is* includes a description of how and why some adults choose to remain single after a divorce and why their choice might make sense for you.

We've also met hundreds of divorced adults who decided that, for them, the way was clear to pursue a new relationship. Among these, we know many who have gone on to form second marriages—or third—that became God-honoring unions, holy and sacramental and inspiring to behold.

Some of the most inspiring marriages we have ever encountered and some of the marriages that most honor God and most reflect His purposes for a husband and wife are remarriages for one or both partners. Far from being a "second best" arrangement or an "inferior" outcome, some of these remarried couples have achieved levels of intimacy, commitment, service to God, and personal and spiritual wisdom that the rest of us would be blessed to duplicate.

While writing an earlier book, *Happily Remarried,* we sat down with a few of these couples to formulate key principles. We learned some healthy habits and best practices that define great marriages—including remarriages. We came away inspired and refreshed by these couples!

In one case, that of Fred and Verna Beffa of Rice Lake, Wisconsin, we were invited to the fiftieth anniversary celebration of a second marriage. It was a second marriage for Verna, and we were invited to help celebrate as that godly, inspiring, wonderful union reached the fifty-year mark. This marriage was meaningful and valuable not only for how long it had lasted but also for how well the marriage had been lived out by these two people!

Choosing to remarry after divorce can lead to a new union that is God-breathed, God-inspired, God-guided, and absolutely wonderful to behold. Just ask the children and grandchildren who were gathered in Rice Lake along with us. There was a lot to celebrate after half a century of watching two Christian adults live their marriage so very well.

This book, then, also includes a description of how and why some adults choose to remarry after a divorce and why their choice might make sense for you.

Are you starting to get the picture?

Intelligent, spiritual, God-seeking adults reach different conclusions as they explore their options after a divorce. This is because each person brings a different life history, a different personality, a different family structure, and a whole different set of values and perspectives into any discussion of the days ahead.

In other words, please don't read this book looking for a definitive answer that instructs you, after a divorce, to stay single for life because it's your only hope.

And please don't read this book looking for a definitive answer that tells you, if you have experienced a divorce, that the best possible choice is to shop around for a new partner and get remarried.

This book is not going to drive you toward one of those two outcomes. We are not going to send you off to a monastery, nor are we going to point you to Facebook and explain how to update your profile to make you more attractive, more youthful, and more desirable to members of the opposite gender.

Your life is your own, and you get to live it.

This book can be an intelligent exploration of your options and possibilities coupled with inspiring examples of choices that other divorced adults have made while traveling the same difficult journey you are on. You will learn from their mistakes and perhaps also from their successes. They are sharing their stories with you for your benefit, for your assistance.

This is what we are doing as well—as authors and family counselors, as students and university professors, as pastors and leaders of ministries to divorced adults, single parents, remarried couples, blended families, and more.

We are reaching out to you to show you a broader, more fully optioned, more interesting world than you might have expected following a divorce. We pray the stories and examples and ideas in these pages will be used by God to help you process your own journey in wise and good ways.

As we were nearing completion of this book, we sat down with a woman who is recently going through divorce. No matter how many times we've done this—hundreds and probably thousands of times—the heartbreak of divorce is always new. The pain is fresh and real. The disappointment and disillusionment are shattering and hurtful. Although we've been through it countless times before, our hearts were freshly touched by this woman's journey and the many challenges she faces in trying to construct a new life.

How will she rebuild her finances? How will she reach out to her children? How will she interact with her family or the family of her ex-partner? Once upon a time these two were one flesh, a husband and wife, active in their church and examples to all of a happy, outgoing couple, filled with hospitality and grace.

Now, in the aftermath of divorce, here is a broken and hurting woman who has more questions than answers, more frustration than joy, more challenges than solutions. Her pain is real, and her situation is difficult.

As we reached out to her, offering comfort and prayer rather than admonishment and instruction, we were reminded of the many other women and men we have met in this exact situation. Now after more than two decades of working with these hurting people, we have had many chances to watch God work—in spite of the damage and destruction.

As we listened to her story, the metaphor of a tornado came to mind. If you are not in a tornado-prone part of the world, perhaps the metaphor of a hurricane would be more on target. Either way, maybe you can get the picture.

After a tornado or a hurricane, there is massive destruction in all directions. No matter where you look, all you see is brokenness and pain. What used to be a beautiful home is now a pile of sticks and bricks, tumbled down and useless. What used to be trees, strong and full of life, are now twisted and uprooted and lying at odd angles and in jarring patterns as far as the eye can see.

Here and there are bits of blankets, or car parts, or clothing—reminders of a house and a family who lived here before the damage was done.

In this bleak landscape of desperation and pain, sometimes the only valid response is to weep and pray. What else can you do?

Yet after more than two decades of working in the aftermath of divorces—or tornados or hurricanes—we can testify that even after massive destruction is left behind, there is still a God, still a Heavenly Father who loves you, cares about you, and is with you even in the dark valleys of pain and suffering.

God stands ready and willing to help you rebuild the walls and replant the gardens and reestablish a sense of family and community life in the days and weeks and months ahead, even after the pain of such great loss.

Maybe life will never be exactly what it once was. Maybe you have lost something precious and valuable that will never be regained. Nonetheless, here you are. And more to the point—here is God as well.

Hand in hand with God you can move forward to a tomorrow that is not marred by fear, scarred by anger, or charred by ruin. Hand in hand with God, you can replant and rebuild and refashion and reconstruct. You can be renewed and revived. You can become new creations in Christ. All this and more is not only possible—it is also God's design for you in the aftermath of the storm.

Storms come, and divorce reminds us of this elemental and immutable fact of life on earth. When storms come, people suffer. But that isn't the whole story.

Grace follows, and grace reminds us that God's abiding love follows us all the days of our lives, even when we walk through the valley of the shadow of divorce. God loves you, and He wants to be your Shepherd and care for your soul.

Within the context of these pages you can explore the contours of God's grace as the Heavenly Father works with divorced adults to create new beginnings, new families, and new hope.

This is what God does—after the storm has passed.

two

ARE YOU FINANCIALLY PREPARED?

As recently as a decade or two ago, a person's credit score was widely considered to be a judgment on his or her character. Employers typically ran routine background checks on potential employees. When they did, one of the primary indicators of personal character was a man or woman's credit history.

A weak or negative credit score was an immediate red flag for lenders and employers. Having a bad credit score meant that a person was lazy, irresponsible, immoral—and possibly all three. Banks and bosses made moral judgments about applicants and borrowers by checking their credit ratings.

Back in that era, men or women with strong credit scores were held in high esteem throughout the broader culture. Such persons were almost universally regarded as ethical, moral individuals. A high credit score told a lender or prospective employer that you were an honest, hardworking and reliable person.

That was then—this is now.

A NEW LANDSCAPE FOR BORROWERS AND LENDERS

In today's depressed global economy, vast numbers of ethical, hard-working, highly responsible men and women cannot find work to replace the job they have lost. These men and women would gladly report for duty and go to work. They would gladly manage their paychecks wisely and budget their monthly living expenses. They would gladly return to the high FICO scores and positive credit ratings they enjoyed when they were employed and their houses were worth more than they owed on them.

The economy has flipped upside down, and the credit scores of millions of individuals and families have flipped also. A decade ago, automobiles depreciated by twenty percent or more the moment the proud new owner drove it off the dealership lot. Houses, by contrast, were reliably expected to gain in value so that a homeowner could steadily build equity and net worth by simply paying the mortgage. In the United States, buying your own home was a key component of the American dream. For most homeowners, the net equity in their homes was the centerpiece of their personal worth.

Now, with homes worth $200,000 or even $400,000 less than the balance owed on the mortgage, homeowners are faced with incredibly difficult challenges.

Ed (not his real name) talked to us about his experience in Henderson, Nevada, an upscale suburb of Las Vegas. Ed has been divorced for eight years and has part-time custody of his two children. He attends a Bible-teaching Evangelical church in the Las Vegas metropolitan area. As he shows us around a single-level suburban home in an attractive neighborhood, he tells us his story.

I bought this house for $450,000 in 2006. At that time $450,000 was the median price of homes in this area. When I bought this house I wasn't stretching or overreaching in any sense to make the purchase or pay my mortgage, taxes and insurance. In fact, my loan officer told me I qualified for a much more expensive home!

Ed sighs with frustration and disappointment.

Today my house is worth maybe $140,000—if I could find a buyer for it—which I can't. None of the sellers in this neighborhood have been able to sell their houses recently. There are foreclosures on my block and many more on the other streets nearby. Right now my mortgage balance is in the high $300,000s. To put it another way, my house is worth a quarter of a million dollars less than the payoff amount of my loan.

Ed looks around to make sure his children, who are visiting him this weekend, are out of hearing range. He continues talking with us but lowers the volume of his voice considerably.

Honestly, the only reason I'm still making the mortgage payment is that I want to keep this house available for my kids as long as I can. I'm not sure how much longer that will be.

Plus, I'm not sure how much longer it makes sense to pay this much money every month for a house that is basically worthless! I would be money ahead to just walk away from my mortgage or even to file a personal bankruptcy.

Ed points to the house directly across the street as he speaks quietly.

One day my neighbors over there just moved out and walked away from their mortgage. My friend Jack down the block did the same thing a few months later. I want you to know I never even remotely considered doing something like that until recently. I'm thankful to still be working, but my company has downsized twice already. The next time I might be one of the employees getting a pink slip.

Every time I pay my mortgage I think I'd be a lot better off to save the money instead of wasting it on a house that has lost so much of its value in such a short time.

I wonder if that's my fault. Should I take the blame for the fact that my house has lost more than two-thirds of its value in five short years? How long should I keep on paying for this messed-up economy?

Like millions of other Americans, Ed is a hard-working, reliable, ethical person with strong moral beliefs. He is a professing Christian and an active church attender. Yet if he loses his job, he will lose his house. Even if he keeps his job, he is actively considering walking away from his mortgage.

Ed wonders if that would be irresponsible or even immoral. He tells us the same thing we've been hearing from many sources as we travel to speak and counsel.

I know a lot of good Christian people who have been foreclosed on or who have had to file bankruptcy. They're good people—in the midst of very bad circumstances. It's a different world out there.

Ed's observation is exactly correct, and it is true in all parts of the country.

In today's depressed global economy a negative credit rating or a difficult financial situation is not an indicator of personal integrity or honor. Instead, we are increasingly living in a world in which good people are suddenly saddled with bad credit. Perhaps you are one of the many Americans who face this same experience. If so, be encouraged by this: you are not alone.

SHEILA'S STORY

Divorced and trying to be a good father for his children, Ed at least still has his job. Millions of other men and women have lost their jobs, leaving them with increasingly difficult choices each month. Pay the mortgage or make a payment against the credit card balance? Which is the greater risk—being forced to move out of the house or losing access to a much-needed credit line on the Visa card?

A recent article in the *Wall Street Journal* reported that for the first time ever, a great many Americans are making their monthly credit card payments the highest financial priority in their budgets. Home mortgage payments are falling to second or sometimes third place—after the car payments. Sheila, a member of a divorce recovery group in southern California, tells us—

I can't give up my car! I need it to look for work. If I end up finding a job, I will need it to get to work.

Right now I am one of those people you're talking about. I make my Visa payment religiously. I pay my credit card bill online, and I pay it quickly. Next I make my car payment, making sure I never get behind. Then, if I have enough money left after that, I pay the mortgage on my house.

At least for now, thank God, I'm able to do that for a few more months. But if I don't get a new job pretty soon, I will probably end up losing my house. If it comes down to that, I guess I'll survive. But there's no way I can live without at least one credit card, and there's no way I can live without having a car.

Unlike Ed, Sheila isn't earning a regular paycheck. She has a house to pay for and children to raise—plus she's making car payments on the vehicle she needs to drive to job interviews. In Sheila's opinion, it is only a matter of time until she loses her house unless, by some miracle, she finds work.

"I do believe in miracles," Sheila assures us, "and right now I sure need one!"

If Sheila doesn't find a job, and if she is unable to keep her house, she will face even more challenges. Typical rentals, whether apartments or homes, require a prospective tenant to supply first and last month's rent, a security deposit, and multiple types of fees to hook up various utilities. A person who has just lost a house is not likely to have several thousand dollars available to put into a new rental. Divorced adults may be especially hard-pressed.

These kinds of pressures sometimes cause divorced adults, especially divorced women, to move too quickly into a new marriages or new relationships. On the surface it appears that forming a new union will bring new income into the household, making children more secure and increasing the financial stability of the family. Notice our use of the term "on the surface." With regard to dating and issues of financial stability, things are not always what they seem.

DUE DILIGENCE WHEN DILIGENCE IS DUE

Sydney Briley, a health insurance specialist in Broken Arrow, Oklahoma, has advice for newly divorced women.

"You should get your own financial house in order before you start dating or get into a relationship," Briley advises. "This way you will not have tendencies to look for a man just to be taken care of."

Briley, who works with a variety of business and individual clients, including divorced women, observes that your potential life partner may not be as financially secure as he appears to be at first glance. "Many men today are not financially secure," Briley notes. "They often have more financial issues than you already have."

Financially stressed and hoping to provide more fully for their children, divorced women may be vulnerable to a prospective partner who spends money freely, including buying gifts or needed items such as school supplies for the kids. These signs of apparent generosity may also be indications of overspending or a personal budget that is out of control. Even when a potential spouse appears to be prosperous, this may be mostly perception. The reality may be much different.

It is neither safe nor wise to assume that marriage will solve your financial problems or improve your credit rating and economic stability. Rushing into a new relationship may bring you a host of problems and issues, including financial ones. It's wise to take a wait-and-see attitude when dating, and it is especially wise to check out a person's true financial and legal status before agreeing to marry.

MOVING TOWARD READINESS: FINANCIAL EDUCATION

One great place to begin is with personal financial education. Among the options you might consider is the well-known "Financial Peace" program developed by Dave Ramsey. The program is offered at many churches as a seminar, workshop, or a series of evening classes. The program receives a constant stream of testimonials from singles, seniors, families, and others praising the system for its ability to get a household on track financially.

Ramsey is a strong advocate of breaking free from personal debts such as credit cards. He advises all adults, including divorced men and women, to operate within a budget and to operate on a cash basis. There is much more to the program, and the study and learning are not the drudgery you might expect! The class itself contains material that is fun and funny. Its goal is to help you feel more successful as you manage your money—or the lack of it. We'll include contact information for the Financial Peace program in the Resources section at the end of this book. You can also do an Internet search for "Dave Ramsey" or "Financial Peace University."

Another excellent resource is a national radio broadcast called "MoneyLife." Currently moderated by Chuck Bentley, this program tackles common financial problems and issues from a Christian perspective. As authors, we have been guests on this program, giving financial advice to single parents. Some of this material is covered in our book for single parents, *Raising Great Kids on Your Own* (Harvest House, 2008). Chuck Bentley is an excellent host, and previous broadcasts are archived on the MoneyLife web site. Again, we'll include contact information at the end of this book.

Your local community college is another potential source of solid help and learning regarding financial matters. Watch the business section of your local newspaper for meetings and announcements. In larger cities there is a constant stream of free seminars and workshops, some including free meals. These are often hosted and led by certified public accountants, certified financial planners, and other professionals. You may be surprised to learn how much help is available to you, even if you feel that managing money has never been your strength.

Whether faith-based or secular, find a money-management approach that works for you and your household. And again, if you're looking for a program that has been field-tested by literally thousands of adults and families, consider the Financial Peace program and related books and material by Dave Ramsey.

MOVING TOWARD READINESS: GET THE PICTURE

There are at least two overall financial snapshots that you'll want to take as you begin to assess your financial readiness. While it is not the purpose of this book to give you specific financial advice or tax information, here are two ways of looking at your financial status. If you haven't done this in detail before, the process can be highly informative and useful to you.

First, sit down and make a very basic statement of your net worth. This is a snapshot that compares the total of your assets (things that have value) against the total of your liabilities (credit card and all other debt).

Assets: If you own a home, that is a major asset and a good first item for your list of assets. If you are fortunate enough to have a 401k or similar retirement program from your employer or another source, list that also. If you own life insurance that has any kind of cash benefit or other value, list the policy.

If you own stock in a company, jewelry that has some value, art that is signed and numbered, or a collection of anything valuable, these are also assets that you would itemize and list as you calculate the asset portion of your net worth. Paid-off automobiles are also assets.

After accounting for all of the major items and categories, you can create a line item of "miscellaneous" and estimate the value of your furniture and clothing, your personal computer, and the other belongings in your household. Be careful not to overestimate this total, but it's fair and acceptable to consider these things as assets.

Liabilities: Now you're ready to work on liabilities. Do you have student loans that are not yet paid off? These are liabilities. Is there a loan against your car? Another liability. Do you pay a home mortgage payment? Another liability. If you're a renter, your monthly rent payment is *not* a liability; rent will show up in the next snapshot you'll take. For now, liabilities are debts you owe. If you have borrowed money from friends or family members, and if you plan to repay that money, add the total of borrowed money to your list of liabilities.

For this first snapshot you will have two lists: you'll have a list of all your known assets, as described above; and you will have a list of all your known liabilities. All that remains is to compare the two totals. Which is larger?

If the value of your assets is greater than the value of your liabilities, you have a positive net worth. Historically, most people who have positive net worth derive it from the rise in value of their primary home. The process used to be fairly simple: buy a house, put some money down at the time of purchase, make regular payments on the house, and gradually you are reducing the balance due on the mortgage. Meanwhile, the house is going up in value, which means you are adding to your net worth over time.

These days, even if you own a home, its market value may be less than the amount you owe on your mortgage. Even so, list the value of your home as an asset. List the mortgage as a liability. What matters is the sum of all your assets versus the sum of all your liabilities. If you have a higher total of assets than liabilities, you have a positive net worth. Congratulations to you!

Despite how you may feel, you are not poverty-stricken. You have a positive net worth. On paper at least, you are in a viable financial situation.

If the total of your liabilities exceeds the total of your assets, welcome to life as we know it in the early twenty-first century. For many persons in North America, divorced or married, there has been a stunning erosion of net worth due to homes losing value, the stock market going down, interest rates declining, and a combination of negative factors that accompany a depressed economy.

If your liability total is larger than your asset total, you have negative net worth. Please do not jump off a bridge or consider yourself a failure. In fact, in this current economic climate, your situation is typical. Look around your church, your neighborhood, and your nation. You are not alone. Vast numbers of people have gone from a positive net worth to a negative net worth during the past decade.

At this point you have one snapshot: a picture of your net worth. This total will change constantly, but you need to calculate it only once or twice a year unless there is a very major event such as the sale of a home, the purchase of a new car, or something similar.

Now for your second snapshot, and it should be simpler. This picture will show your monthly reality—or cash flow.

You'll compare the total of what comes in with the total of what goes out. You probably already have a general idea of how this is, but you may be surprised when you get down to the details!

Once again, you'll make two columns. In the first column, write down every source of income that flows into your household during the month. If you happen to receive alimony or child support payments, these are sources of income. For the purpose of the snapshot, assume that you receive these payments on a regular and timely basis. If you are employed, write down the total take-home pay you receive during the month. For the purposes of this snapshot, don't worry about your gross income and taxes. That kind of study can wait until you're doing your tax return at the end of the year. For now, just focus on the total amount of money that finds its way into your bank account during the month.

Other sources of income to include on this list might include part-time jobs, government assistance such as AFDC or other programs, and anything else that provides you with money during the month.

In the second column make a detailed list of where your money goes. Begin with the easy parts: major items such as rent or mortgage payments, car or student loan payments, credit card payments, utilities including cell phone and cable television, and all your other regular recurring monthly bills. Use a typical or average month, not a month with exceptionally low or unusually high utilities.

Now for the hard part. To make this snapshot accurate, you'll need to understand what you spend on things like gas, groceries, coffee, fast food, the occasional movie rental, and similar expenses. Many of these items will be small expenses that you probably don't keep track of. Even so, it's time to make a serious and sober-minded estimate of what these costs are.

Until you get a financial education as described above, try to be as accurate as you can. How often do you pick up a taco on the way home? How often do you have coffee somewhere while you're out? What is your typical weekly grocery bill? How much gas goes into your car in an average month? If you pay for child care or if you spend money regularly for a baby-sitter, include those amounts as you make this list. Basically, every time money leaves your bank account, that's an item to track for this snapshot.

As you did before, compare the totals of your two columns. One column has all the income you receive during the month; the other contains all the ways that money flies out of your household during the month.

How do the two columns compare? If during an average and typical month you receive more money than you spend—congratulations! You have positive cash flow. Having positive cash flow makes it possible for you to move forward. Positive cash flow is how you make progress financially.

If during an average and typical month you spend more money than you receive, you have negative cash flow. This makes you normal. But just because it's common doesn't mean it's wise. Consistent negative cash flow is why your credit card bills keep climbing; you are borrowing money that you don't have in order to keep living the way you currently live. This is not the American dream—it's the American reality.

Getting these two snapshots in place—your net worth and your monthly cash flow—can be absolutely liberating, even if the news seems negative. The pathway to a brighter financial future begins with a solid understanding of where you've been and where you are today. Without turning this chapter or this section into a lesson in financial education, let's just say that these two snapshots are the simplest way to get a handle on how things really are for you as a divorced adult.

Got the pictures?

If so, we're ready to talk about the next part of assessing your readiness.

WHAT'S YOUR SCORE? FICO AND SIMILAR RATINGS

Fair Isaac Company (FICO) developed one of the first numerical ways to compare the credit standings of various persons. Based on a sliding scale from about 300 on the low end to perhaps 850 on the high end, Fair Isaac crunches financial data about your employment, place of residence, past and current debt obligations, past and current payment patterns, and produces a number that guides banks and lenders in determining how to evaluate you as a credit risk.

These days there are other companies offering similar services, and some larger banks have their own forecasting models that produce scores that are comparable to the original FICO model. The exact process by which you are assigned a FICO score remains shrouded in mystery, and the process has been adjusted and refined as consumer behaviors change and as the larger global economy shifts from positive to negative, as it has recently. The FICO scoring process is not static; it is continually reevaluated and improved so that credit forecasts are as accurate as possible.

One of the key factors in most systems involves the relationship between how much credit you have available—the credit limits on your various credit cards—versus how much debt you have right now. Are you at or near your credit limit on most or all of your credit cards? If so, this will negatively impact your FICO score. Conversely, if you keep your credit card balances at less than half of your available limits, this produces a positive report that results in a higher score.

Some people have made a science of balancing their available credit so that each card is at or below the key fifty-percent borrowed ratio. This behavior appears to have a very positive impact on your credit rating.

Are you a safe risk because your income is high, your debts are low, you've held the same job for a long time, and you haven't moved recently? If these things are true, and if you have a pattern of paying your bills promptly and keeping your credit card balances low, you'll have a FICO score on the higher end of the range.

Have you moved recently, lost a job or changed jobs, or gotten behind in making payments such as a mortgage or car payment? These have historically been negative indicators on the scoring model, resulting in a lower number for your FICO or other rating.

The way in which divorce affects your credit score varies in every case, but there are few general overall patterns. In today's economy, divorcing couples tend to fight over who will assume responsibility for the joint obligations and debts rather than who will receive control of the shared assets. If one of you has a great deal of debt in his or her own name before a divorce happens, the other partner may actually experience an increase in his or her credit worthiness when the marriage ends.

One way or another, most lenders want to consider your credit worthiness based on a comparative numerical score. If you've never heard of this process, or if you would simply like to know where you stand, you can access a great deal of data and information by going online to <http://www.myfico.com>. You should always access such sites from a secure computer rather than a computer in a public place such as a library, hotel lobby, or anywhere multiple users go online using the same computer.

NOT REQUIRED: PERFECT ECONOMIC HEALTH

If every person waited until he or she was completely financially secure before getting married, the wedding business would dry up in a hurry. Even though today's parents often insist that their children wait a while until they're on a more sound financial footing, the reality is that few of us will ever be entirely ready for marriage in sheer economic terms. Still, there is often wisdom in waiting.

Do you need to put off dating until your net worth reaches a certain level? No, but it certainly helps to be tracking your net worth as described above. And if your net worth is significantly negative, you would be wise to get solid financial advice before thinking about dating and relationships.

Perhaps there is a Christian debt-restructuring or credit-repair business in your area. Despite frequent misdeeds among companies of this type, there are some genuine ministries available that can help you improve your financial situation and increase your net worth and your qualifications for receiving credit.

Do you need to put off dating if your monthly cash flow is negative? In general, yes. As Sydney Briley commented earlier in this chapter, it is wise to get your own financial house in order before considering a relationship. You may need to manage and control spending, obtain and secure a steady income, and repair or improve your credit rating or credit score. These are steps toward better health.

Your goal should be a confident and accurate assessment of your personal financial situation. Even if your overall economic picture seems bleak, it is so much wiser to know where you stand than to ignore how things are. Confidence is built and hope begins to float as you realize exactly where you are and as you begin to take small steps to improve your financial stability.

For many divorced adults, and particularly for divorced women, one of the attractions of a new relationship is the prospect of more income, a higher standard of living, or better care for your school-age or younger children. For some, the desire to get out of a cramped apartment or a low-income housing situation may also hold huge appeal. Divorced adults of both genders often dream of returning to a house-in-the-suburbs lifestyle, yet combining two poverties rarely produces this result. This is why it is so important to get your own financial house in order and, as we'll discuss in the next section, to get a realistic picture of your potential partner's financial health and wellness

To sum up, you do not need to be wealthy or well off before you consider dating or marriage. However, it is certainly wise to be healthy and well-informed and moving forward toward greater financial stability before you do any serious dating. When you are financially "needy"—or needy in any other way—you are more vulnerable to rushing into an unhealthy relationship or agreeing to a new union before you've carefully considered the wisdom of such a decision. When you feel confident about your financial situation and about your ability to plan and order your financial life, you are much more likely to have a mature, eyes-wide-open approach to dating and remarrying. Gain confidence first; consider relationships later.

YOUR POTENTIAL PARTNER: GETTING THE PICTURE

There's no easy way to say this, so we'll be blunt. As we've worked with divorced adults across the past two decades, we find a clear trend among men and women who are dating and considering a new marriage to misrepresent themselves, putting their best foot forward, minimizing or downplaying their liabilities or past mistakes. If you absolutely must hear it plain and simple: *sometimes people lie.*

Is this new information for you, or have you already found it so?

Melanie's new husband was more than $80,000 in debt on their wedding day, but he hadn't mentioned it.

"I have a car loan and a couple of credit cards, but it's nothing I can't handle" is how Melanie remembers her new husband talking about his financial status while they were dating. Since she knew he had a good job and was making a high income, she didn't worry when he talked about a car loan or having more than one credit card balance. After all, everyone has credit cards!

"I couldn't believe it," Melanie tells us in the parking lot of a large church. "I mean, this guy is $80,000 in debt, and he can't find a way to tell me that *before* we get engaged and before we get married? Not only that, but I happen to know he spent $3,000 on my ring, which I didn't need. Do you think I would have let him spend that kind of money on me if I'd known he was already $80,000 in debt?"

Melanie shakes her head in disgust and continues:

I'm just so mad at myself. Why didn't I insist on getting a credit report on him? My best friend told me to do that—she had been divorced and had remarried. But I just blew her off. I knew Robert was working, and I knew he got paid well, so what else was there? I was so naive.

Melanie looks at us as we write down her comments and adds with strong emphasis,

You put this in your book—you tell divorced women they should get a credit report on their potential husbands and maybe do a full background check also. Tell them they need to look at the documents, not just take somebody's word for it! Tell them about my mistake, and then tell them not to do what I did.

She pauses.

Don't be fooled by the fact that he's working at a good job or appears to make good money or spends a lot on you or on your children. Look past all that and get down to the details.

I'm not going to leave him. But I'll be honest with you: if I had known he was in this far in debt, I wouldn't have said yes.

IS HEAVY DEBT A DEAL-BREAKER?

In a small-group survey of fourteen people taking a divorce recovery class, a dozen raise their hands in response to this question: "If you found out your potential new partner was heavily in debt, would that keep you from getting serious about the relationship?"

Twelve out of fourteen raise their hands and vote yes. Yet answering a question in class is much different than becoming attracted to someone, starting to get to know him or her, thinking about marriage, and then finding out there's a serious financial issue such as high debt.

One of the two abstaining class members offers her perspective.

I don't think the other person's financial picture is really what matters. To me, it's more important whether he's honest about it. I think if I love somebody, and he's honest with me, we can probably work things out together. So for me, knowing someone was heavily in debt wouldn't be the factor that kept me out of the relationship.

Lying to me is what would stop me from going forward with someone. I've been lied to before; in fact, my ex was a world-champion liar, and I didn't know it for a long time. So as far as I'm concerned, if a guy lies to me, he might as well hit the road. We're not going anywhere.

But if he has problems in his life—maybe financial problems or maybe problems with his kids or whatever—and he's honest about it and doesn't try to hide things from me, I would stay in the relationship until we figured out whether getting married was the right thing to do.

Around her, several class members who had raised their hands were wavering in their previous opinions. One of them, the youngest divorced female in this group, is ready to change her vote.

I guess I agree with that. Maybe I was too quick to judge someone by their financial situation. I put my hand up because I have a lot of debt myself, and the last thing I need is a partner with too much debt. No way! We'd be doomed from the start.

But after listening to Carrie, her opinion makes sense. Why should I rule someone out just because he has financial problems? She's right; if a guy is honest with me, I would probably not walk away just because of his high debts.

We're tempted to vote again after these statements, but we defer. Instead, we frame a question that underlies much of what we've been saying in this chapter: "For you personally, do you make character judgments about someone if you find out he or she has a lot of debt or has bad credit?"

The group discusses this at some length.

The conclusion is this: bad character hides problems and is dishonest. Good character is open and honest, even when there are serious issues. So debt or a bad credit rating is not an issue of character. The character issue is whether your prospective partner tells you the truth and admits his or her problems.

YOUR OWN READINESS: RISE OF THE DEBIT CARD

Financial planners who work with divorced adults point to a steady and consistent negative impact on finances when things aren't going well for a person or a family.

Jack, a certified financial planner in Orange County, California, puts it this way as he discusses the negative impact:

> You know things are bad when you are charging your basic monthly expenses such as gasoline and groceries because you don't have adequate funds to purchase those necessities. You whip out your credit card for twenty dollars' worth of groceries or twenty dollars' worth of gas. That may seem like an insignificant amount at the time, but it's deadly.
>
> You're so stressed out financially you don't have even small amounts of cash to make your smaller purchases. This is how credit card debt spirals out of control. Everybody thinks it's about big splashy purchases such as new furniture or new clothes or a new car, but for most people,

their finances really head for a fall off a cliff when they're using credit cards to pay for small everyday purchases.

Gradually they get used to doing that, and it's the biggest trap known to mankind. If you don't have twenty dollars to get a few groceries on the way home, then what you should do is not get groceries right then. I know that may sound harsh, but it's the best advice I could give someone in that situation. Put this in your book: *just don't do that!*

Happily, North American consumers are taking Jack's advice. The most recent data from banks and consumer groups indicates that people are still turning to plastic for everyday expenses, but now it's the debit card that rules.

Debit-card use for everyday purchases has been on a steady uphill climb since the global economic downturn began. As people pay down credit cards and use credit less often, they are simultaneously ramping up their use of debit cards at places like gas stations, convenience stores, and supermarkets. Unlike credit cards, debit cards involve spending money you actually have. You won't be paying interest or penalties or late fees; you're simply spending the money that is in your account.

Jack observes that there a few traps in that as well.

Some banks will approve your debit transaction even if you don't have money in the account. Then they charge you huge overdraft fees because you exceeded your balance.

They try to say it's your fault, but, after all, who approved the transaction? I would support legislation in Congress that requires banks to turn down a debit card purchase if the funds aren't available.

It would be far better for the consumer if the transaction just didn't get approved. That sure beats letting the purchase happen, then getting a high fee slapped against your account because you're overdrawn. I could tell you stories of things I've seen the big banks do that you wouldn't believe. So even with a debit card, which I advise all my customers to use, you still need to be careful.

Tell your readers to know how much money they have *before* they spend it with a debit card. Put that in the book too.

THE REVIEW BEFORE THE QUESTIONS

We'll close this chapter with a set of questions that can help you assess your financial readiness to consider dating or remarriage. But first, let's summarize the primary points of this current chapter.

First, it's important that you know your situation. Step back and get the bigger picture about your finances instead of letting your emotions rule. Take a rational, thoughtful, deliberate approach to finding out where things stand.

In this chapter we proposed two quick snapshots. The first was figuring out your net worth, even if that amount proves to be negative. Whatever it is, your net worth is a key indicator of your financial health. For readers in the United States, you can take some comfort in knowing that the average net worth per capita has been declining steadily for more than five years, mostly a result of the decline in home values.

Second, we proposed calculating your monthly cash flow. This may seem tedious and difficult, but it's worth the effort. The only pathway to riches that is absolutely certain is this one: every month, spend less than you earn. If you do that consistently over time, you will build financial stability and wealth.

So before going forward, it's wise to figure out what your monthly cash flow is.

You may be thinking, *What cash flow?*

Yet the exercise is valid, even if you are unemployed and don't appear to have an income. The truth is, you are still spending money, aren't you? You are still paying rent, perhaps a car payment, insurance for your car, your health, and your life. You are still buying groceries and maybe getting fast food occasionally. So it helps to gain a bigger picture by calculating your monthly cash flow.

It's also helpful to know your current FICO or similar credit score, a number that banks and lenders use to determine your worthiness to receive credit. This number can affect obvious things—the interest rate on your mortgage or car loan—and can also affect less obvious things such as how much you pay for insurance on your car. In many states, persons with low credit scores are put into a "high risk pool" for car insurance, which means paying rates as much as three times higher than what a normal risk person would pay.

So whether you know it or not, your FICO score matters.

We talked at length in this chapter about getting a good, solid financial education. Every adult should do this; it is vital for every divorced adult. One option we recommend, and mentioned earlier, is the Financial Peace program by Dave Ramsey. There are other programs and other options available, but find something that works for you. A program or a plan that helps you gain control over your own financial situation and circumstances is very helpful.

Work on improving your own financial life before you worry about dating and relationships. Get a handle on your spending. Watch your net worth begin to increase, even if it stays in negative territory for a while. When your net worth increases, you may find your confidence increasing right along with it.

If you are already dating, pay no attention to whether someone spends money on you or your children. His or her free-spending ways may not mean wealth—but possibly just the opposite. What's important is that anyone you seriously consider marrying should be honest and forthright with you about his or personal life and especially about his or her own financial situation.

Many divorced women echo what many financial planners advocate: before you agree to marry someone, get a credit report and possibly a background check. This may seem cold and calculating, but let the misery of others warn you against making a big mistake. Too often divorced adults are naive and trusting, just when they should be wary and careful. Don't let this turn out to be you!

Are we advocating that you defer dating or remarrying until you're wealthy and successful? Not exactly. But you should definitely defer dating or marrying until you've taken a good, long look at your overall situation. You should work on getting your own house in order before setting up house with someone else! You should build your own confidence in managing money, planning a budget, and making financial decisions.

Become the leader you need to be instead of hoping for a new leader to come along and manage your financial life for you. Learning these new skills will benefit you and your children both now and in the long term. Whether you stay single or choose to remarry later, learning to master money and manage your finances is a life skill that adds value and virtue to your journey.

Questions for Your Personal Study and Reflection

1. After following the instructions in this chapter for calculating your net worth, answer this question: do you have a positive or a negative net worth? Is this what you expected to discover, or is the outcome a surprise to you?

2. After following the instructions in this chapter for calculating your weekly or monthly cash flow, how do the "income" and "expense" columns compare? Do you have a positive or negative cash flow? Is this what you expected to discover, or is the outcome a surprise to you?

3. Do you know your current FICO score? Have you kept track of your score over time so that you know what direction it is moving in? Has your FICO score changed since your divorce? If so, has it moved to a better score or to a weaker score?

4. Do you understand that your FICO score is impacted by how promptly you pay your bills and by how wisely you use your available credit? Do you realize that keeping your credit accounts at half the available balance or below will strengthen your FICO score and increase your credit-worthiness?

5. Has your own financial status shaped your ideas about dating? If you are in a serious relationship or will be in the future, will you be willing to disclose your financial situation honestly and transparently? Why or why not? Would you expect a potential life partner to disclose this same level of information to you, prior to making a decision to marry?

6. Have you ever considered pulling a credit report or running a background check on someone you were dating? Why

or why not? Does this advice seem overly harsh or suspicious to you, or do you understand why some counselors, ministers, and others highly recommend this step?

7. How would you answer the same question that was posed to the divorce recovery class in this chapter: "If you found out that your potential new life partner was heavily in debt, would this affect your decision to marry or the timing of your marriage to this person?"

8. Do you agree or disagree with this statement? "Bad character hides problems from other persons; good character is open and honest with others."

9. Have you cut back on your use of credit cards, switching over to debit cards or cash for most of your transactions? Why or why not? If you tend to have a balance owing on your credit cards, is that balance increasing each month, or are you actively paying down your debts, including credit card debts?

10. Have you taken a financial education class such as Dave Ramsey's? If so, did the class impact the way you think about or use money in your daily life? What changes have you made to your financial behavior since getting this education?

three

ARE YOU EMOTIONALLY PREPARED?

"Don't use my real name!" she begged us, so we agree to call her "Jackie." Jackie attends a large independent church in a suburban area and has been recommended to us by the leader of a divorce-recovery group in the area.

"You should talk to Jackie," the ministry leader tells us. "She has a story that would be quite helpful for all divorced women to hear." When we press for details, the wise ministry leader defers—"You should really hear that from Jackie herself. Let me give you her contact information."

So a few days later we're sitting outdoors with Jackie, and she begins her story.

> He really knocked me off my feet. I had been divorced for about eighteen months and was busy rebuilding my life, praying about going back to school for more education. Meanwhile, I attended a divorce recovery group at a big church near my home. In the weekly classes I found help, hope, sage advice, and also some new friends.
>
> One of those new friends, a divorced man I'll call Bob, quickly became more than a friend.

We had sex the first time we went out. I have to tell you, I didn't see that coming! It's not like I was taking the class to meet someone. Anyway, since I met this guy in church, I guess I assumed we both had the same basic values. And the way I grew up, you didn't have sex until *after* you got married.

Even so, the very first time Jackie and Bob went out on a date, they had sex. How did that happen? *Why* did that happen? Jackie fills in some of the gaps.

He took me out to a Mexican restaurant I dearly love. He asked me where I wanted to go, and he let me choose the restaurant. The restaurant I chose is not the most expensive place in town, but they make a spinach enchilada that is absolutely my favorite thing! So I told him about the restaurant and about the spinach enchiladas, and the next thing I know we're sitting at a table, eating chips and trading stories. He had me laughing one minute and crying the next. I really didn't say much because he was so talkative.

Bob told Jackie about an ex-wife who had never really understood him and had apparently been having serial affairs throughout their entire marriage. When he eventually discovered that his wife was sexually involved with his best friend at church, Bob decided enough was enough, and he sought a divorce.

His story was so sad. I liked him already, but the more we ate and the more he talked, I just kept feeling sorry for him. I felt that he had been through a lot and he had been hurt a lot. Even though I didn't know him yet, I found myself caring about him and wanting to help.

As the meal concluded, Bob offered to show Jackie the apartment complex he lived in, part of a large upscale development. There was no mention of seeing Bob's actual apartment. In fact, Bob's stated motive was to show Jackie the complex in case she wanted to move there in the future.

He told me it was a perfect place to live. He told me about the great gym and workout facility and that there were seven separate pools. He said the people who lived there were quiet working adults—exactly the kind of neighbors I would want to live near.

Although it seems obvious in retrospect, Jackie didn't sense that Bob was coming on to her or trying to get her over to his own apartment for other reasons. She accepted Bob's statements at face value. She was unhappy with her current apartment, a noisy building on a busy street. The idea of moving and having an on-site workout facility was intriguing.

Having already treated Jackie to an enjoyable dinner at her favorite restaurant, Bob was the perfect tour guide as the two friends strolled around the apartment complex just as the sun was setting.

It was a beautiful evening. At that point everything had been perfect, Jackie recalls.

We walked around all seven pools, we thoroughly explored the different areas of the fitness center, and by the time I was walking back to my car, Bob was holding my hand, and it felt natural and safe. Bob suggested a quick look at his place, and I agreed. Even then it didn't seem like a pick-up line. I went to his apartment to see the layout of the rooms.

And, as they say, the rest is history.

Several patterns here are familiar to us as family counselors. Perhaps the clearest one is how a divorced male can quickly win the sympathy of a new friend. Bob sat at a dinner table and quietly told a tale of being hurt by an unfaithful wife. He filled in a lot of details and seemed fairly honest about his previous marriage. Yet step by step, Bob was invading the caring heart of a kind and godly woman.

Women tend to be naturally gifted with empathy and concern; these God-given capacities can be exploited—consciously or unconsciously—by men hoping for a conquest. Since we don't know Bob's actual motives on that first date, we won't assume that he was deliberately trying to woo Jackie into his bed. Maybe that outcome was a complete surprise to both of them. Or maybe not.

Jackie looked down at her feet as she went on with her story.

I'm not saying he raped me. I knew what I was doing, and I knew in my heart that it was wrong. I don't know why my usual barriers and defenses weren't working that night. I don't know why I went along with him. But I do know that I could have stopped it from happening.

Jackie is quiet for a while, and we allow her some privacy.

A young mother walks past us, striding briskly as she pushes a double stroller. We can't help looking at the stroller's occupants, twin girls with curly blond hair and matching outfits. Both girls are soundly asleep.

We tell the passing mom that her babies are beautiful.

She smiles in response. "This is the most peaceful part of my whole day," she explains to us. "The rolling motion of the stroller always puts both of them to sleep. It never fails!"

We smile and the young mom resumes her brisk walk.

Jackie sighs as she watches the twin girls disappear from view.

I could have gotten pregnant. It's not like I was taking birth control at the time. I was single, and I hadn't had sex in about three years. I wasn't prepared to end up in some guy's bedroom, making out with him and then having quick but passionate sex.

Less than a month after that first date, Jackie moved in with Bob, more or less permanently. Since the lease had not expired on her own apartment, Jackie didn't change her legal address or file any related documents. But in all functional ways, she no longer lived in her former apartment; she now resided at Bob's.

The two continued attending a large Evangelical church. The messages continued to be Bible-based. The worship experiences kept on being positive and encouraging. Jackie and Bob began openly talking about getting married, yet when it got down to specifics, Bob would get vague.

I could never pin him down on a date or even a basic timeframe. But we talked about it, and sometimes he would ask me if I wanted or needed some new jewelry for the occasion. He never seemed defensive or hostile on the topic of getting married. I allowed myself to be convinced that our marriage was only a question of when, not a question of if.

Living together, sexually active, not married. Jackie and Bob fit a profile that is exceptionally common in churches today, even Evangelical, Bible-teaching churches. A quick survey of pastors at a large conference recently affirmed that each pastor finds much the same situation in his or her own context.

"It's not just the kids anymore," one pastor commented. "It's the divorced adults, forty or fifty or sixty years old. Some of them are still raising kids; some of them have grandkids. What kind of example do these adults think they're setting?"

The pastor allows his question to trail off into space. Beside him, another pastor chimes in.

"For couples thinking about a remarriage, I can't remember the last time I sat down with a couple who weren't already living together. There they are in my church, week after week after week, yet they are sexually active and not married."

Four months after their first date, Jackie and Bob were living together and still not married. Bob had offered Jackie an engagement ring—if she really wanted one—but told her that he wasn't ready to set a date.

"He always had a plausible reason why we couldn't get married quickly," Jackie remembers as we watch a couple of rabbits nibbling on grass nearby. The rabbits are grazing their way up a shady slope near one of the waterfalls.

"Bob is so rational, and so wise in many ways, that I always trusted him when he brought up whatever reason we couldn't marry immediately. Meanwhile, he kept on discussing it. He offered to buy me a ring, and I kept on believing that sooner or later we would walk the aisle together. Somehow, that made it okay that we were living together before getting married."

Until one fateful Sunday when their young pastor preached about sex.

Our church has two lead pastors, one older and one younger. One Sunday the young pastor was preaching, and he got on the topic of couples living together and how that displeases God. Here he was, this young guy who seemed very plugged in to our culture and very aware, and he got all wound up on how couples living together are sinning and God is not happy.

Jackie pauses briefly in her narrative.

I sat there blushing like a schoolgirl. I hope nobody was looking at me during that sermon, because I could feel my face get hot, and I knew it was beet red. All of a sudden, all of my rationalizing and all of my excuses and all of my "we're going to get married later, so it's okay" kind of went right out the window. I knew I was living in sin, and I wanted out.

Jackie went home from church and began packing her things. Her apartment lease had not yet expired, and she was still paying rent on her apartment.

I had moved all my clothes and things over to Bob's place. I don't know if I would have found the courage to quit living together if God hadn't given me that way out. I had a place to go—I was still paying rent there—so I just moved out.

Jackie worried that Bob would stop her from moving out. Strangely, he made no attempt to do so. He asked Jackie what she was doing; after she told him, Bob left the apartment for a few hours and did not return until after Jackie was mostly packed. At no time did he try to prevent her from leaving.

I was completely moved out by that same Sunday night. It only took me three loads. I got the last load unpacked into my old apartment, and I sat down in the middle of the floor and cried. I don't even know why I was crying or what I was crying about.

I cried like a baby for a while, and then I prayed to God and asked Him to forgive me for living in sin. Then eventually I tried to fall asleep. I laid there wondering what came next, whether Bob and I were still a couple or what.

Unknown to Jackie, the relationship with Bob had ended when she announced she was moving out. Bob would no longer communicate with her, return her texts or calls, or acknowledge her existence. He quit attending the church services they had attended as a couple. Although he remained in his same apartment, for all intents and purposes, Bob had dropped off the map.

Jackie continues quietly.

> It was almost a year later before I found out the truth. What I found out was that the whole time Bob was living with me in his apartment, he was still married to his wife.

> He had lied to me about being divorced. Looking back, I wonder how much of the rest of it was a lie. Did he really have a wife who cheated on him? Did she really get involved with his best friend at his former church? I'll probably never know those answers. All I know is, not only was I living in sin sexually, I was also living with somebody else's husband. I'm angry about that, but mostly I'm mad at myself. I can't believe I fell for it. I can't believe how stupid I was.

Later, as we talked with Jackie about why she became involved with Bob, common themes begin to emerge, none of which involve stupidity on her part.

First, Jackie explains to us that she was lonely after the divorce. She missed her husband, even though the marriage they shared had never been a romantic, deeply intimate union.

> I missed having someone around the house. I missed having someone to talk to. I missed having someone to help me with chores in our home. I went from living at home with my family to being married and raising a family. I was never alone that whole time. Now, suddenly, after the divorce became final, and with the kids all grown and gone, I was all alone. And I was definitely lonely.

Second, Jackie realizes that she didn't have a plan for dating.

I hadn't made a decision to date. I was still trying to make up my mind about that. So I didn't have a strategy. I hadn't thought about what my boundaries would be. I hadn't developed a plan for dating. In my mind, I wasn't planning to date for a while, so I didn't need a plan. The whole thing with Bob grew out of a class we shared together at church. Even when he asked me out, I really didn't think of that night as a date. So I was unprepared.

Third, Jackie tells us that her long absence from sexual union left her surprisingly vulnerable to romance—not sexuality.

You may not believe this, but here it is. That first night with Bob, after our dinner and after walking around the apartment complex, what would have meant the world to me would have been someone to just hold me, maybe hug me. I would have been more than fine with a kiss. Honestly I wasn't looking for sex—or even hoping for sex. Not at all!

I was absolutely thrilled when he reached out to take my hand. I loved it when he held me. I enjoyed it when he kissed me.

I would have been just fine if it had ended there. I wish I could have found the courage or the will or the presence of mind to just stop it there. We had sex that first night, but it wasn't the sex that left me encouraged and fulfilled. It was the fact that someone had held me, talked to me, and taken me out to dinner. It was romance I was hungry for, not sex.

You may not believe that, but it's exactly how I felt. And of course I also realize that even if we'd stayed away from sex—and I wish we had—Bob was still married to someone else, and he was still hiding his marriage from me. No matter how enjoyable romance is, I do not want romance with someone else's husband. Not now. Not ever again. I want romance from a single man or from no one at all.

Also I'm not going to date—with or without a plan—until I know I'm ready for it. I've been taking a good long look at myself and some things I need to work on as a person. Until God and I have worked on some of those things, I am not in the market. End of story.

Jackie's tone of voice displays a decisive confidence. She has made up her mind on this matter.

THESE EMOTIONAL PATTERNS MEAN YOU'RE NOT READY

With Jackie's story as a backdrop, let's look at some familiar patterns that occur among divorced adults, both male and female, before they're emotionally ready to consider dating. We see these patterns repeated in younger adults and in older ones, in adults with children and in adults who never had children. While these patterns are part of your life, you are wise to postpone dating.

If you find yourself in some or all of the following patterns, this is a good time to realize that you are not emotionally ready for the beginning of a new relationship. Maybe someday, maybe later—but not right now.

NOT READY PATTERN 1: THE ABCS

We work with various types of therapy, including cognitive processing therapy and cognitive behavioral therapy. We work with an always-changing official manual for diagnosing patients. These manuals are numbered sequentially (such as DSM 4, DSM 5, and so on). For the purposes of this book we are going to set aside the technical jargon and speak in plain language.

After a divorce, one of the most common emotional patterns we encounter is one we label the ABCs: anger/bitterness clusters. A vast cluster of emotions that encompass rage, frustration, hurt feelings, jealously, and so forth—emotions that we can categorize as anger or bitterness—tend to inhabit the emotional landscape of a divorced person. ABCs can vary somewhat in the way they are expressed; the common denominator is a high level of frustration or resentment.

If you find yourself divorced and also angry, we can diagnose that quickly: you are normal. You are typical. You are a functioning human being with the normal and usual responses that a human being has when a relationship ends. It is natural and normal to be angry, frustrated, and upset. It is also—strategically speaking—not the best time to consider starting a new relationship. Not right now. Not while you're angry or bitter or frustrated or hostile. These emotional markers are telling you that it's wise to work on your own issues before dealing with someone else.

Before allowing yourself the possibility of a new relationship, it's time to do the hard work of sorting out your own ABCs. Sit down with a trusted friend or close family member. Sit down with a clergy person or a lay ministry leader.

Consult with a professional counselor. You don't feel ashamed if you see an ear, nose, and throat specialist or a chiropractor. When you have a specific area of need, you make an appointment with a professional who specializes in treating that need. It is exactly the same with counselors. Counselors specialize in emotions and behaviors. If you want to work on emotional issues, sit down with someone who specializes in emotional wellness.

The beauty of talking about these issues is that you can begin to make some progress toward health and wholeness. The advantage of talking with someone who has training in these areas is that you can become more self-aware and recognize and admit your feelings for what they are and waste less time in unhelpful denial. With the aid of a trained counselor or qualified pastor, you can make faster and better progress.

Having said that, recovering your emotional health is not a race, and no one—including you—should have a stopwatch out to time the process. Relax and quit worrying about whether you "ought to be over it by now." There is no guideline that fits all persons or all situations. Each one of us is emotionally unique, and each one of us faces unique challenges. You don't need to get healthy "faster"—you need to get healthy more deeply, more genuinely, more completely. It's not a race.

There's no need to race through your ABCs so you can reach the finish line. Take the time you need to recover from anger. Talk through your pain with a friend or a counselor, someone who can listen and give wise advice.

Instead of denying or repressing your ABCs, let them breathe. Expose them to God's truth. Talk about them in group settings if that will be helpful. Before you know it, these unhelpful emotions will have far less power over you. You'll begin to break free from the toxic poisons of bitterness, resentment, and rage.

NOT READY PATTERN 2: LOL

Contemporary social networks use "LOL" to mean "laugh out loud" or also sometimes to mean "lots of love." When *we*

for a while—not counting a sense of irony or bitter humor, which doesn't qualify as part of this particular marker.

One clear sign that you're on the road to recovery is that you've found your laughter again. You have the ability to laugh at yourself—and you do. Friends and coworkers notice a smile on your face more often. You laugh out loud with your children or the lunch crowd at the office. Life is fun and funny again.

Obviously, not everyone is outgoing. Not everyone is the life of the party before a divorce—let alone after one. Yet as you begin to genuinely recover from the emotional trauma and psychological scarring of a divorce, the natural contours of your sense of humor begin to reemerge. You return to previous patterns of hearing and telling jokes, noticing and commenting on funny situations, and more. Whatever was once normative for you in the way of humor returns and begins to thrive.

In fact, recovering from divorce often increases your ability to find the humor in daily life and to laugh out loud more often. Jenny, divorced after more than two decades of marriage and raising three children to college age, found a sense of humor that was greater than she had known while married.

It took a while, but as I began to get better, I started to realize how tense I had been during the last three years or so of my marriage. I lost my laughter during the marriage, not as a consequence of my divorce. I spent the last three years of my marriage frightened and tense and not sleeping well. I wasn't myself—and I had almost forgotten who I really was.

As I really started to recover from the divorce, I laughed like I had not laughed for a long time. I wasn't holding back all these repressed feelings. I wasn't tense and upset and afraid. My worst fear, which was that I would end up divorced, had actually happened. Yet here I was! I had survived my worst nightmare and found out that I would really be okay.

That made me able to laugh again. I wasn't trying to recover my sense of humor—it just happened that way. My friend Donna from high school, who had stayed in the same community and lived nearby, told me she hadn't seen me this happy since we were teenagers.

I took that as a high compliment! It meant that I really was starting to get better. I wasn't moping around all day feeling sorry for myself. I was smiling and laughing and relaxing more often. I was spending more time around positive people.

Jenny's story resembles that of many divorced adults who move past feelings of loss and abandonment only to discover that their former good nature had been there all along, below the surface, waiting to come back.

When Jenny says that she had almost forgotten who she was, that is exactly what we are talking about in this section. One clear indicator that you are recovering your emotional health is that you laugh again, smile again, and start resembling the younger you.

It's a change that your friends and family will notice. If you pay attention, you'll notice the change too.

So go ahead—smile at that person in your mirror!

MARKER 2: YOU'RE FEELING MORE CAPABLE

All of us have strengths and weaknesses. No one is good at everything or capable of everything. This is true whether we are single, married, or divorced.

Somehow divorce can affect the way we feel about our own capability and competency. If you're a divorced woman whose husband has always repaired the car or managed the finances, you may begin your divorce experience by feeling inadequate in these tasks and incompetent in some key areas. If you're a divorced man whose wife has always done the cooking, cleaning, and laundry, you may feel as though you need some basic life skills all of a sudden: you don't know how to do anything! These feelings are normal and are somewhat rooted in basic truths.

As you begin to recover from divorce, you also begin to discover some new capacities within yourself. You may discover that a "real man" can iron his own shirts, wash his towels, and cook his meals. Quite a few divorced males become gourmet chefs after a divorce; it's not a requirement, just a frequent outcome. Divorced men often discover a real flair for cooking even though all they've created during their married life was toaster waffles or Saturday morning pancakes. Now, alone and without a live-in cook, men discover they enjoy mixing ingredients, experimenting with new flavors, and making a huge mess in the kitchen.

Divorced women often discover that they enjoy learning how a car works and how to take care of it. As we'll talk about more fully in another chapter of this book, divorced women often enjoy learning more about finances and managing money. Before, these experiences were taken care of for them, and the women appreciated the fact that their husbands provided these services. Now, however, divorced women find that they enjoy learning.

"I can change a flat tire!" one divorced woman told us. Bev was in her late 40s and had never even filled her own gas tank.

Now, without a husband around, she was learning to put oil in her car, change a flat tire, and why it matters that she check tire inflation on a regular basis. As this woman began to tell us about her learning experiences, we could see and appreciate her obvious pride in learning these new life skills.

It can be the same for you. At first you'll be intimidated and overwhelmed by what you can't do, by what you've never had to do during your married life. Then, gradually but consistently, you'll discover that a washing machine is not a total mystery, or a Ford F-150 is not actually operated by rocket science, and you'll apply yourself to tasks and problems that you never cared about before. You'll grow in your knowledge and in your capabilities.

Out of that growth in ability should also come some significant growth in your feelings of competence and capacity.

"Now if something happens to me on the road, I know how to handle it," Bev told us. "It's not like I want something bad to happen, but if it does, I know what to do now. I don't need to be afraid of my car breaking down when I'm driving it all by myself. I know what to look for, and I know what to do!"

Bev's journey is a perfect indicator of Marker 2—feeling more capable. It's a good sign that you are healthy and on the road to recovery.

MARKER 3: HEALTHY SELF-ESTEEM AND PERSONAL CONFIDENCE

Many adults who experience divorce end up dealing with deeply rooted feelings of embarrassment or shame. These adults feel that they are somehow a disappointment to their parents, family, children, or friends. They internalize a true statement—

my marriage ended—by granting it exceptional emotional leverage over them—which means *I am a failure.*

As marriage therapists and family counselors, we have worked with adults even three or four decades after a divorce—who still feel ashamed of themselves. These adults see divorce as an evil and themselves as stained by failure, even when it was their life partner who ended the marriage, ran away with the secretary, or chose to have an affair instead of being true to the marriage vows.

Shame is a powerful emotion, rooted in our own understandings of morality, spirituality, and values. Generally speaking, we do not choose our feelings of shame; instead, we are often surprised by them and perhaps a bit overcome. Shame weighs down on us and convinces us that we are different, defective, and unworthy.

Yet there can be hope in the midst of trauma and even shame.

If you've ever shopped for or purchased a new car—let's say a Mustang—you immediately begin to notice something. All of a sudden you start seeing Mustangs everywhere! They're all over the road. When did this happen?

The Mustangs were there all along and in the same quantity, but you didn't notice them until you started paying attention. Once you got interested in owning a Mustang, or once you drove a new one off the dealer's lot, suddenly you began noticing what was around you all along—a lot of Mustangs.

As you recover from divorce, the same effect works to your benefit. Before you got divorced there were a great many divorced adults in the world, but you didn't notice them the way you do now. After the initial shock and awe—"divorce has happened to me"—comes a new revelation. There are a lot of divorced adults in the world. In fact, divorce is happening all around you, both inside the church and outside its boundaries.

Shame begins to ebb as you realize that your own experience of divorce has a broader context: there is a lot of divorce happening. As family counselors and authors, we wish the world were different. We wish divorce were rare or even nonexistent. We wish every marriage lasted for the lifetimes of its partners.

Yet the truth is this: there are a lot of divorced people in the world. You know this fact subconsciously, but you don't fully realize it until you cross over and become a divorced person.

One of the clearest markers of emotional healing is when we discover that we've moved past our feelings of shame and our sense of inadequacy. We can admit out loud that our marriage ended without adding the false tag line that means "I am a failure." The reality is that a great number of immature, unhealthy adults can currently list "married" as their relationship status. And a great number of healthy, wise adults must currently list "divorced" as their relationship status.

There is no correlation between marital status and personal maturity.

Divorce is what it is. Divorce means something has ended, something we valued and treasured and hoped would last forever. It's over now, and we miss what we once had. Yet as we recover from the emotional trauma and impact of divorce, we realize that we are human beings like everyone else. We are not worse or better or different than other people. We are just people.

As you heal and recover, you begin to return to a healthy sense of confidence in yourself and a balanced sense of optimism about the future. You are not a failure; you are not fundamentally incompetent. You are what you are: a person who has experienced the end of a marriage, and with God's help you have managed to survive and move forward. In the same way—with God's help—you can and do look toward a future that may include your best days ever and your highest personal achievements. Divorce hurts, but it will not keep you from following God, and it will not keep you from accomplishing many good things in your life and family.

Somehow as you heal, a realistic but buoyant sense of self-confidence begins to replace your feelings of shame and inadequacy. You are not boastful or proud, but neither are you shy and afraid. You have survived a trauma, and you are coming out the other side stronger and healthier and better prepared for the life ahead.

Your sense of loss and grieving is gradually supplanted by a sense that better days are ahead—days filled with wiser choices, healthier patterns, and happier outcomes in relationships.

Questions for Your Personal Study and Reflection

1. Using a scale from 1 (lowest) to 10 (highest), how would you assess your own ABC level? When you think about your ex-partner, the divorce, or your current challenges, do you often find anger rising up in your thoughts and feelings?

2. Have you consulted with a counselor or minister to help you process your feelings of anger so you can move forward to better emotional health? Have you poured out your heart with a trusted friend in order to help release your emotions and move forward?

3. To what extent is LOL (loneliness issues) a part of your daily life? Do you feel you have access to a supportive network of friends and family who are with you in the struggle, or do you feel that you are usually all alone to face the difficulties and to solve the problems?

4. If you are raising children, to what extent do you hide your feelings from them in order to help them stay more positive? Conversely, do you find yourself dumping on them and letting your negative emotions flow out during mealtime, drive time, bedtime, or at other times? Why is this so?

5. How much time do you spend blaming yourself for the divorce? Do you feel personally responsible, in whole or in part, for the end of your marriage relationship? Whom have you discussed this with in order to gain a more realistic understanding of your own innocence or blame?

6. One of the adults quoted in this chapter talked about feeling like a failure. Have you ever felt this way—like a failure?

Do you understand the difference between saying, "My marriage failed," and saying, "I am a failure at marriage"? Which statement comes closer to how you feel and speak?

7. Are you spending more time with your close friends lately? Why or why not? Are you making time to be with the people you care about just so they know you still care about them? How do you accomplish this?

8. Who among your family members seem to understand and perhaps even relate to what you are experiencing right now? How often do you text, e-mail, chat by phone, or talk to them in person?

9. Do you allow discouragement to keep you away from church and the things of God, or do you find yourself encouraged and uplifted after attending a worship service or church ministry event?

10. Ultimately, who is responsible for how you feel? Regardless of what happens to you in the external world, who should be responsible for what happens in your inner self, your thoughts, your feelings?

four
ARE YOU SPIRITUALLY PREPARED?

What happens to a woman's faith and spirituality when she suddenly finds herself abandoned by her husband, served with divorce papers, and facing the prospects of raising her kids by herself? Where is God while all of this is happening, and why doesn't He intervene to change the whole situation for the better?

What are the spiritual and religious outcomes when a family shatters and a mother and father begin to live separate lives? Are there trends we can track and report regarding faith and spirituality? Are there typical results that can help us define the process and categorize the spiritual effects of divorce?

The simplest place to begin is to recognize the following: divorce is like a train wreck, causing extensive damage strewn in its wake for many miles in all directions. It's like a hurricane tearing through a coastal community with powerful destructive force. No matter how you analyze it, divorce is a disaster, plain and simple. Divorce hurts, and it leaves plenty of pain in its wake.

If you have ever experienced a divorce in your life, no one has to tell you about all the damage and destruction. You have witnessed these things yourself. You can testify about all the negative energy unleashed by a divorce. You can describe the harmful effects that divorce has on children, relatives, extended family members, friends at church, and others.

You already know that divorce harms and that divorce hurts.

What you may not be prepared for is this: divorce, despite all its inherently negative and harmful impact, can also be a catalyst for amazing spiritual growth and remarkable personal transformation. From the ashes of divorce can rise new life, new wisdom, and a new person. Without being simplistic or formulaic, we'll look at how and why that's possible as we consider some real-life cases.

SHATTERED AND ALONE

Martin pastored a small church in the Southeast, part of a wide swath of the United States often referred to as "the Bible belt." Martin enjoyed pastoring; it was the fulfillment of a lifelong calling for him. He found purpose in preaching, teaching, and helping people answer the deep questions of life and spirituality.

Although his church was not large, Martin liked to believe that people were finding hope and help in the midst of life's many challenges. He liked to believe that his ministry was making a difference in the community in which he lived. He baptized new believers, received new members into the church, and occasionally performed weddings and funerals. He administered the sacraments and especially enjoyed the traditions and rituals of Holy Communion, surrounded by other saints.

Then one crisp winter day Martin's wife surprised him by filing for divorce. She had already made her decision, consulted an attorney numerous times, and made plans for a new life without Martin.

Completely unprepared for any of this, Martin found his entire life in disarray. And as he quickly discovered, the end of his marriage was also the end of his pastoral ministry.

Even now, Martin talks about that dark period in his life with obvious emotion and sorrow. Several times during his narrative, he stops to regain his composure and struggles to find his voice. To this day, many years after these events, Martin is still affected and impacted by the pain he experienced when his marriage ended.

My church was as supportive as possible. Several people offered to reach out to my wife, although she wouldn't meet with them or even deal with them at all. And a number of people there, especially the men on my church board, spent a lot of time praying with me and asking God for His guidance and His direction for my life.

Despite the best efforts of many, Martin's marriage could not be saved. His wife filed for divorce, seeking primary custody of the children. Martin, trying his best to be Christlike and to represent the church well, did not argue or contest his wife's choices and decisions. With the wisdom of hindsight that is available to him now, he might have done things differently. But in the midst of this completely unexpected crisis, Martin struggled just to get up in the morning, just to have his personal prayer time, just to find meaning in the Scriptures or in the familiar practices of his faith.

Meanwhile, his wife turned away from God entirely, announcing that she no longer believed in Christ or the Christian message. She refused to meet with any of the women of the church or a delegation from the church board, or even with friends she knew in the neighborhood and the community. Martin says of his wife,

> She was angry. She was mad at the church, she was mad at God, and she was mad at me. She closed herself off and wouldn't let anyone—not even her parents or her siblings—inside.
>
> So much anger poured out of her when the divorce happened. She told me I had been unfaithful to her—that the church had been my mistress and my other woman. She told me that she felt unloved and lonely and that I spent all my time loving other people while neglecting her.
>
> What shocked me so much was that she had never once mentioned any of this during our marriage or during my ministry. It's not like we had this discussion regularly and she pointed out what I needed to work on or what I needed to change.
>
> Instead, she kept all these things bottled up inside her and never shared them with me. I didn't hear any of this until she had already consulted an attorney, started some paperwork, and put the divorce process in motion. I was completely unprepared for this! I knew we weren't the most intimate of couples, and I knew our marriage wasn't perfect, but I thought our life together was pretty normal and that our relationship was more or less okay.
>
> It was not until the very end, after her mind was already made up, that she started saying all these things about feeling abandoned and neglected and about the church being

sort of the other woman in my life. Hearing this all at once, never having heard it before, not having a chance to respond . . .

Martin sighs loudly and leans back in his chair, studying his hands.

I was hurting so much at the time that I didn't even realize there was some truth in her words. There was much validity in her perspective.

Martin is suddenly very silent, and the counselor does not interrupt the quietness that has momentarily filled the room.

At the time, I wasn't the husband God wanted me to be. I was pouring myself into the life of the church and into the lives of the people in the church, but I wasn't deeply investing my heart and my energy into my wife or my marriage.

He looks down at the floor.

The truth is, I wasn't a good husband during those days. I wasn't loving or attentive or kind and considerate. I was a very good pastor, but as a husband, I wasn't honoring God or cherishing my wife. I didn't see it then, or I would have tried to improve, but I was emotionally detached from my wife and my children. My whole heart was invested in trying to make the church a healthy, growing, successful place. I needed success—and the church seemed like my one shot to achieve it.

I blew it. God gave me a wife and a family, but I wasn't smart enough to take good care of them. When I think about it now, I realize I have no one but myself to blame for what happened.

After finishing his confession, Mark slumps backward in his chair.

THE SCARLET LETTER: "D" FOR DIVORCE

At the time of Martin's first pastoral tenure, divorce tended to be a career-buster for those in ministry. Most churches gently but firmly insisted that a pastor who experienced divorce while serving in ministry should step aside immediately. Many believed that the existence of a divorce disqualified someone from serving in any type of spiritual leadership or public ministry role.

"If he can't manage his own household," some said openly about Martin at the time, "then how can we expect him to manage the things of the church?"

Martin's church board, while privately supportive of him and offering him prayer and encouragement, nonetheless insisted that he would be better off if he left the pastorate while the church searched for a new minister to lead them.

RISING FROM THE ASHES

We've included Martin's story in this chapter because his life exemplifies the positive potential that exists in the midst of something negative: a divorce. Martin lost his job, his income, his identity, and also his wife and marriage. Although he continued to have limited access to his children, he wasn't able to be the kind of father he always hoped to be.

Although Martin had hoped to stay close to his children, both emotionally and geographically, what actually happened was that he moved three states away from his ex-wife and her new partner in order to take the only job that seemed to be available to him. Martin insists he had no agenda to leave town or get away.

My sister's husband managed a cell phone store. I couldn't find a job anywhere in town, and one day I was talking to my sister on the phone, which I was doing a lot as the divorce unfolded. She asked me to think about coming out there and joining her husband in the cell phone store. Frankly, I didn't have any better offers coming in.

Five months after losing his wife and his ministry, Martin moved to a new community and took a commission job as a salesman, selling wireless phones and various Internet plans. He discovered that he enjoyed working with people and that his skills as a pastor made him a good sales-closer. Within a few weeks of starting the new job, Martin was consistently among the top cell phone salesmen for his company in the regional territory where he worked.

Imagine that! All that seminary training and all those courses in Greek and Hebrew, and I ended up selling people new phones and wireless plans. I stood in a tiny store all day and just talked to people. But I found out I was good at it.

Martin, who more than anything needed self-confidence and direction, took heart in having high sales figures. He also enjoyed earning more income than he had ever made while pastoring—even though the terms of the divorce eventually required him to send most of his income to his ex-wife.

I didn't need much to live on. I was renting an apartment on a month-to-month lease, and I didn't have a life. All I did was go to work and come home. I watched entirely too much television.

It was almost a year after losing his marriage that Martin began to experience what he now describes as a crisis of faith and a turning point in his life.

I woke up on my wedding anniversary, and somehow all the sadness, all the despair, all the unfairness of it just hit me like a truck.

I called in sick to work, but I wasn't sick. I sat at home at my depressing little kitchen table and just stared into space for a long time. I asked God where He was and where He had been while my marriage was ending. I cried a little bit, and I don't cry very much. I don't know why it took a year for things to hit me like that, but all of a sudden it was like I took a great huge punch in the chest. It knocked the wind out of me, and I couldn't catch my breath for a while. I guess I kind of hit bottom that day.

Depressed and angry, Martin reached for a Bible and began to read. He half expected to find a chapter where God explains why divorce happens and how to make everything better, as if by magic. Instead, he now believes he was guided by his Maker to a much more appropriate place to begin.

I picked up reading where Paul talks about all the things that happened to him—beaten, shipwrecked, stoned—and I realized, maybe for the first time, that bad things really do happen to good people. Just being in ministry didn't give me any kind of exemption from bad things happening. The more I read about Paul, the more I realized my situation wasn't as desperate as his. He had people trying to kill him! All I had was this huge sense of personal failure and a deep hole in my heart where my wife, my kids, and my ministry had once been.

That day became kind of a starting-over point for me. That day helped me wrap my mind around a huge fact: my marriage was gone forever. My kids were going to grow up in someone else's house. The future for me was going to look a lot different from the past. And it was up to me whether or not I wanted to include God in that future.

Martin sighs and shifts in his chair for a moment before continuing.

I remember praying that same day, asking God if He would give me another chance at a wife and a family and telling Him that I would give it my very best effort. I would be the kind of godly husband and godly father I needed to be. I told Him I didn't need to be a pastor ever again but that I was willing and available if He could use me.

I told God a lot of things that day, but mostly I told Him I was sorry for the mess I had made of my life and that I was ready to start over. It was kind of like a conversion experience. It was a rebirth for me—or the start of one.

Fast forward to today. Martin pastors a growing church in the suburbs of a large Midwestern city. He's been in pastoral ministry at this church for a number of years, and the church has grown steadily during his ministry.

When we mention these things to him, Martin visibly recoils.

Yes, the church is growing now. But I need to tell you that in serving here, my focus is on my wife and my marriage, her kids, and our kids. I make that my first priority, right after serving God. The church comes after God, after my marriage, after my family.

You could never have convinced me that putting my marriage ahead of the church would actually grow the church! All those years I invested my energy in trying to grow a church—while I lost my family. Now here I am, making my wife a priority and our kids a priority, and somehow the church is growing by itself. I tell you the truth: I have no idea why our church is growing.

It seems completely backwards to me, but that's what is happening here. The more I try to be a good husband and a good father, the more the church seems to grow. It makes no sense, but that's what we're seeing.

HOW WE GOT HERE

After several years of selling cell phones, Martin discovered that he was missing the pastorate. He missed preaching, he missed hospital visits, he missed dedicating babies and performing weddings. He missed almost everything except maybe the church board meetings.

Martin was ready to explore a return to the ministry if a church would have him. Was there a church anywhere that would consider having a single man—a divorced single man at that—serve as the pastor of their congregation?

Would the baggage from his past prevent him from having a future?

These thoughts and others flooded Martin's mind as he talked to a former seminary professor, a friend or two from his ministry days, and his sister. He was asking all of them the same question: "Can a divorced guy get a job as a pastor?"

The answer—in Martin's case—was yes.

As he began to reach out and make connections, he heard about a district superintendent who had installed several divorced men as pastors of churches on his district. Although Martin didn't know this DS personally, he liked what he was hearing. Here was someone in church leadership—a district superintendent—who was actively placing divorced persons into roles of leadership. *Could this be true?*

Martin took a leap of faith and called the DS one autumn afternoon. He recalls,

> It was a slow day at the store. I had learned to watch the ebb and flow of customer traffic, and I knew we wouldn't get busy soon. So I picked up a cell phone and entered the number of this DS I had never met. I don't know why, but he answered my call on about the third ring. That by itself is amazing!
>
> We talked about a half-hour on that first call. I told him I was the one at fault in my marriage. I told him my wife had an affair, but she did so because I was emotionally distant, and I wasn't caring for her needs. I told him that my kids were being raised by another man in another state, and I was lonely. I told him that I still felt called to preach, but I wasn't sure God wanted me.
>
> I was more honest with that guy on that call than maybe I've ever been with anyone in my entire life. I didn't even know him, but somehow it seemed safe to just pour it all out and tell him how it was.
>
> At the end of the call, he asked if he could pray for me. He wasn't promising me a job or a place to pastor, but he wanted to just pray and ask God to bless my life and ask God to open doors for my future.
>
> I think, for the first time in my life, I was experiencing the grace of God. For the first time, I was encountering God's mercy, God's love, God's grace—all of that wrapped up in a district superintendent I had never met who just wanted to pray and ask God to bless me.

When I hung up from that phone call, I didn't know if I would ever pastor again. I didn't know if I would ever be married again. But I did know one thing: *God loved me.* And I knew God was going to be involved in my life and my future.

That phone call was the start of a whole new life for me and the beginning of every good thing God is doing right now in my personal life and also in my ministry here on this district.

CATASTROPHE OR CATALYST

The impact of divorce has a dual nature with regard to our spiritual lives and our faith. First and foremost, divorce often causes us to question everything we've believed about God and His goodness. *If God is so good, why are bad things happening to me, and why are bad things happening to my children? Doesn't God love my kids? Isn't God compassionate and kind? How could a compassionate God allow my spouse to totally destroy our family?*

This kind of questioning, coupled with a negative outlook on life or a cynical approach to evaluating others, can cause us to separate ourselves from God and from the community of faith—perhaps permanently. Many who experience divorce flee from their former friends and abandon the congregation where they once participated in worship and ministry as an intact family. The stigma of a shattered family causes many to withdraw from fellowship entirely.

It is not uncommon for divorce to lead to a crisis of faith and for the crisis of faith to result in the loss of formerly held beliefs. This outcome is avoidable, in part by the church "being the church" with regard to those who experience divorce.

For far too long, those who are victims of divorce have been treated as outcasts, separated from the warmth and fellowship of the faith community. Ironically, as the need for fellowship increases, the opportunity for fellowship may decrease.

Terry Glaspey, an articulate Christian author who writes about C. S. Lewis and other subjects, observes that the church is often ill-equipped to serve and help those who are coping with the effects of a divorce. "We don't understand other people's experiences," Glaspey notes. Safe in their intact marriages, well-intentioned churchgoers may fail to connect with the uncertainty and anguish a divorced man or woman is working through. The church may offer programs for divorce recovery—a commendable effort—when what is truly needed is the incorporation and inclusion of divorced adults within faith-filled social and personal networks.

Isolation from the community of believers is toxic to spiritual life and health. John Wesley, whose affirmation of small accountable groups of Christ-focused disciples led to the founding of the Methodist movement, believed that authentic spirituality is best formed and best served in community. Conversely, without the community of faith in which transparency and accountability are practiced and upheld, spiritual health suffers, and spiritual growth sputters to a halt.

Separated and feeling alone, many divorced adults question their faith and never move forward toward meaningful answers. Instead, they spiral downward into depression and anger, unable to escape the fog and haze of shattered illusions.

Yet there is another possible outcome, one that Terry Glaspey suggests as a valid and desirable alternative to despair and frustration.

"Divorce can be a chance to reboot your life, spiritually and personally," Glaspey observes. "Divorce can open up the opportunity for genuine spiritual transformation."

One divorced churchgoer describes her spiritual life during the years of her marriage:

I was coasting. My husband and I were both active in ministry and occupied positions of leadership, including service to the key boards and committees that governed the church. Yet I felt neither passion nor commitment in my Christian faith.

I came to church, I listened to the sermons, and I tried to do my part when people asked me to serve. Yet in my own soul there was mostly stagnation and paralysis, nothing like intensity or authenticity.

A literate and well-read person who has taught English at her local community college, this woman continues with a wry observation.

While I was married and our family seemed normal, other people looked up to me, which I didn't deserve. I wasn't the spiritual giant others may have assumed I was because of my leadership roles in the church.

But the funny thing is, when my husband left me and I got divorced, it felt as though everyone was looking down at me, which I also didn't deserve. As I struggled to understand my divorce and why all this was happening, I began to really grow in my spiritual life for the first time. I became an authentic follower of Jesus Christ, and I began to read the Scriptures because I wanted to, not because I felt guilty after a sermon. Is the world upside-down or what?

It's a question well worth considering. For many adults, divorce sets in motion a process of transformation and growth, leading to a faith that is passionate and authentic, perhaps for the first time. The contours of this pathway may follow several key markers, which we'll discuss in the paragraphs that follow.

MORAL INVENTORY AND PERSONAL RENEWAL

Participants in the Celebrate Recovery movement, many of whom battle to overcome addictions and addictive behaviors, move through several defined steps in their journey toward better health. One of these, generally listed as Step Four in the growth chart, involves making a moral inventory that is "searching and fearless."

How many married adults, busy rushing from one commitment to the next, actually take the time to make a searching and fearless moral inventory? It's not exactly a high priority inside or outside the church. Life is a rush of raising kids, paying bills, coping with challenges, and gradually getting older. In such a setting, who has time—or cares deeply enough—to undergo an intentional process of soul-searching and self-discovery? The unexamined life may not be worth living, but it is highly normative for married adults in twenty-first-century Western culture.

Divorced adults, on the other hand, suddenly encounter an iconoclastic experience that tears down many of their personal defense mechanisms. The carefully constructed sense of self and self-worth, often shaped and defined by marriage and family, is now in shambles. From all the wreckage, what will emerge? Will the real me please stand up and be identified?

When a wise adult allows the trauma of divorce to impel a searching and fearless moral inventory, the result can be a newly realistic sense of self. The outcome can be a sense of identity rooted in more accurate understandings of who I am—not as a husband or wife, father or mother, parent or child but as a person standing in the need of God and His presence.

True humility can grow here, while the former vestiges of pride can be shrugged off and set aside. All forms of pride are deadly, but spiritual pride—based on an exaggerated sense of one's maturity—is lethal. Divorce raises the prospect of overcoming pride, resisting the temptation to think too highly of oneself, and moving forward in gentle, truth-accepting humility.

After more than two decades as family counselors, serving more often inside the Church than outside of it, we can affirm that some of the most spiritually mature persons we have ever met are adults who have experienced divorce. Somehow these perceptive men and women allowed the trauma of divorce to help them pull back the masks of false spirituality and exaggerated maturity, revealing an honest glimpse at the person inside. Instead of simply looking into the mirror and then striding away unchanged, these men and women let God begin to do His work in their hearts and lives, undergoing radical transformation in their personal character.

THE LIBERATED SELF: NO MORE PRETENDING

Sunny and optimistic, Shelley shatters the perception that divorce can leave a woman bitter or cynical. One who smiles easily and laughs often, she talks about how her own divorce led to a radical change in her spiritual life and also her basic personality.

Divorce was liberating for me. Please don't think I'm recommending divorce or suggesting it to someone, because I'm not, but I need to testify about how divorce worked for me.

Before my divorce, my spiritual life was mostly about performance and behavior. When I was going to church, when I was praying for people, when I was reading my Bible—not that I was ever great at those kinds of things— then I felt good about myself. I knew God loved me, so I enjoyed church when I was doing well spiritually.

But you can see the problem with that, I'm sure. When I wasn't doing well, when it had been a long time since I read my Bible or when I wasn't praying for people very often, then I felt bad about myself. I felt I didn't measure up to God's standards. I felt like God was disappointed in me, so I tended to stay home from church and not come into God's presence.

Shelley stops again before continuing her narrative.

Let's take the really big one: Witnessing. I was guilted all my life about witnessing to others. If I wasn't witnessing to others, then I wasn't a good Christian. So for most of my life—because I wasn't doing evangelism or passing out tracts or whatever—I felt bad about myself spiritually. I had this sense of what a good Christian was, and I knew I didn't measure up to that.

When my divorce happened, it shattered everything. While I was working through all my questions and yelling at God and everything that goes along with that, all of a sudden I encountered a God who loved me. And this God didn't love me because I was Super-Christian; this God loved me just for who I was, His child—His daughter.

Shelley smiles widely and looks across the desk at two counselors.

"Have you ever realized that?" she asks with the wide-eyed innocence of a school-age child. "Have you ever gotten to that point in your spiritual journey when you realized that God loved you? Not because of stuff you were doing but just because you were His kid, His joy, His delight."

Shelley leans back in her chair, relaxed and happy.

I never got that before. I never got that when I was married. Maybe I could have, but it just wasn't how I was formed. It wasn't how I grew up. I grew up in church being constantly told to pray, read my Bible, and especially to be out there witnessing to people. And since I never was great at any of those things, I never really liked myself spiritually. And I assumed God didn't like me either.

Then I got divorced, and I couldn't possibly measure up. So I had to kind of start over with everything. I had to figure out who God was and what He wanted from me. I had to figure out how to relate to God as a divorced woman and not as a seemingly successful married woman.

The result of all that is this: I know God loves me now. God loves me and I know it, and that changes everything. I don't have to pretend anymore. I don't have to fake anything. I don't have to behave or perform or measure up. God loves me just the way I am.

Shelley is not a theologian, and she isn't trying to be. She's just a woman who grew up in the church but never really understood God until she looked at Him, and herself, through the broken lens of divorce. There, for the first time, she saw the contours of grace outlined in the face of a loving Heavenly Father.

ADVERSITY AND CHANGE: THE ROAD TO CHARACTER

A veteran missionary to China was asked why the Christian Church had grown so swiftly there—while underground— when it seemed to be in decline in the Western world. Sitting in a suburban living room in the United States, the elderly statesman was quick with his response.

"In China there is constant adversity and suffering, but in the West Christians have an easy life filled with material comfort."

He continued:

> You should know this. In China we pray for you, because perhaps your life is more difficult. You in the West are distracted and always entertained and very comfortable, so you lose your way. We in China must focus, and we must endure hardship. The result is that we pay more attention to our Christian walk, and we grow in our understanding of Christ and His many sufferings.

A book about divorce may seem like a strange place to quote a long-term Christian missionary who served for most of his adult life in China. Yet there is a meaningful connection between this man's observation about spiritual growth in persecuted places and our chapter about spirituality and divorce.

"Tribulation produces perseverance," is how Paul explained this phenomenon to the young church at Rome; "and perseverance, character; and character, hope" (Romans 5:3-4). In this strategic chapter of the Book of Romans, Paul is explaining the role of adversity in producing godly character, which was exactly the point of the Christian missionary's exposition and precisely what we are talking about in this section of a book about divorce.

Hardship and adversity are prime opportunities to form good character, moving beyond childish ideas into a fully-formed faith. Divorce, which brings us more adversity and hardship than we could have imagined, can become the catalyst for learning endurance, perseverance, steadiness and—yes—hope. Who among us wouldn't prefer an easy life, given the choice? Yet divorce robs us of the choices we might prefer to make: we enter into a reality that is not of our own choosing. There in the hardship we discover that God is real, that enduring is possible, and that our experiences can form us into wiser, more mature believers and persons.

DRAWN TO THE DIVORCED

This brings us, by round turn, back to Martin, who pastors a church as he leads a blended family together with his second wife. Martin, who experienced a divorce and lost his ministry, has also experienced grace and returned to ministry with a new awareness of life's purpose and meaning.

He tells us,

> One reason our church is growing is that we seem to be attracting people who are divorced. Maybe other churches are experiencing the same thing; I don't know. What I do know is that our church is especially welcoming to people whose marriages have ended or whose family life has been less than perfect.
>
> People walk in here, and although I don't exactly shout it from the pulpit every Sunday, it doesn't take long for people to discover that there is divorce in my background, that I am a remarried person, and my wife and I are blending a

family. So if your life has been messy and you walk into the door of this place, you feel right at home.

Martin shrugs his shoulders.

Am I glad people are getting divorced? Of course not! Who could possibly be glad about that? What I'm happy about is that when people do get divorced, which they do, there's a place where they can feel accepted and valued and loved and worthy. Our church is not perfect, but it's that kind of place. We are a welcoming place, an accepting place. We have a lot of people with messy backgrounds and messy lives, and we are all kind of growing up together, doing life together, learning what faith means together.

Maybe that's what the church is supposed to be. Or at least that's what some churches are called to be. I honestly feel that our church is carrying out a divine mission. I truly believe that God has formed us this way, to reach those whose lives aren't perfect, those who are hurting and hopeless.

SPIRITUAL GROWTH FIRST, RELATIONSHIP LATER

Sitting together around a table in the church basement, a group of divorced women are quick to offer advice about spiritual growth after divorce. "Get your own issues sorted out first, and then worry about dating later," says one woman who is taking her own advice. "Figure out who God is, and figure out how serious you are about God, and then relationships will find their proper perspective."

Around her, other women nod in agreement.

"I think if you put God first, that's the most important thing," says one woman who is now dating after being divorced for eight years. "I think I wasn't ready to think about dating in those first few years after my divorce, when I wasn't sure if God was real or what I believed anymore. Back then I had so many questions that I don't think I was ready to get into a new relationship. I needed to find my way back to God and make Him my first priority."

"And your kids your second priority," opines another woman at the table. "That's exactly the right order. Get things worked out with God, and get your kids into the rhythms of a whole new kind of family life—then worry about men later."

The women laugh out loud at this remark.

"Or don't worry about men at all," says one woman to more laughter.

The point is well taken.

While you are recovering from a divorce—a process that doesn't happen in neat stages or yield to orderly timetables—explore your faith and work out your understanding of God and His grace. Find a fellowship where you can plug in and receive; then later plug in and give back. Find a church that is a place where broken people fit in and feel included.

As your faith journey unfolds, don't be too quick to fall for a new partner or explore a new relationship. Instead, develop a mature, adult relationship with the Father you have in heaven. Give Him a chance to rework your priorities and make over your identity; allow yourself plenty of room for questions and ambiguity. Explore what faith means for single persons, divorced persons, people like you.

"When you're really right with God," one woman at the table comments, "You can trust God to worry about whether you're ready for a relationship. You can leave it up to God as to whether or not He puts someone in your life. You don't need to be on Facebook trying to find a new friend."

The women laugh again at this comment.

"Amen," says one woman to nods of approval.

The voice of experience speaks clearly and reveals much wisdom.

Questions for Your Personal Study and Reflection

1. In your experience, how did your church fellowship—if you had one at the time—respond to the fact of your divorce? Did you feel supported and encouraged by the church and its leaders, or did you feel isolated and unworthy?

2. In general, how would you rate the Christian community on reacting to divorce and people who are divorced? What is the Church doing well? Where does the Church really need to step up its game and do a better job of helping people cope with divorce and its aftermath?

3. Think about the best sermon you ever heard on the subject of divorce. Why was that sermon helpful? How did it help you grow in your understanding of God, marriage, or the future? Who preached it, and how recently?

4. Have you fully embraced the fact that while God hates divorce because it causes so much pain, He does not hate divorced people?

5. In general, would you say that your divorce has brought you closer to God, moved you farther away from God, or hasn't had any impact in that regard?

6. In general, would you say that you have increased in spiritual maturity since the divorce, or would you say that you are probably moving backward or downward in your spiritual life since your marriage ended?

7. Did your divorce raise questions in your faith? Did your faith in God weaken or waver after your divorce? Did you re-

think God's sovereignty—His power over situations and circumstances—after your divorce?

8. If you knew of a church that was led by a divorced pastor, would you be more likely to attend that church because of his or her divorce? Conversely, would you be less likely to listen to this particular leader because there was a divorce in his or her background?

9. If a pastor is divorced and then remarries, would you listen to that pastor's opinion on family matters? Would you regard that pastor as stronger or weaker as a leader and minister given that kind of experience?

10. What books are you reading right now that are helping you grow spiritually and move forward in your faith? What books are you planning to read in the near future for the same purpose?

five
ARE YOU PHYSICALLY PREPARED?

"I wasn't sleeping at all," Kelly remembers, talking about the weeks and months after her husband walked out of her life. "I would lie down to sleep at night and try not to think about my husband. But all I could think about was him, where he was sleeping, who he was sleeping with, whether or not he would ever come back to me, whether or not he would come back to his kids."

Kelly shakes her head.

At that time, I still didn't understand what was happening to me—to us. I guess that's a common reaction, but it was all new to me. I kept thinking that it was a bad dream and that I would wake up one morning and he would be in bed next to me where he belonged and that all of this was just a nightmare.

I honestly believed that he would come to his senses, end the affair he was having with a woman who was also married, and get back to living his real life. In those first few weeks and months after he left me, I was clinging to false hope.

This is Kelly's narrative, not ours. She is the one who has reluctantly concluded that her hope was false and there was no point in believing her husband would one day return to her. However, after more than two decades of working with divorced adults, we can assure you that this is the story of many other women who are abandoned by their husbands.

"My kids kept asking me questions," Kelly recalls. "They would ask me things like 'Is Daddy coming back to us?' and 'When will Daddy come home?'"

She pauses a moment to regain her composure.

I had no idea what to say to them. I had never read any books about divorce, because I never thought that information would apply to me.

My kids had all these questions, and so did I. I wasn't trying to lie to them or hide things from them, but I had no idea of what was happening or how long it would go on, or what the outcome would be. I felt helpless as a mom and as a person. What was I supposed to say to two young kids and a son who was almost a teenager? How was I supposed to help them process the fact that their dad was permanently splitting up our family and messing up all our lives?

I was so unprepared—so completely shocked and surprised by what happened, and I was totally unaware of what divorced people and single moms have to cope with every day of their lives.

Looking back, I wish I had been more helpful to others while I was still married. I didn't know how good I had it back then. I didn't understand how challenging it was—how incredibly difficult—to raise kids on your own.

We're chatting with Kelly about her physical health in the days immediately following her divorce. Like many other men and women who have seen their marriages come to a sudden end, Kelly found herself in a downward spiral emotionally and spiritually but also struggling with physical symptoms.

I didn't sleep at all. I tried taking sleeping pills, which I really don't like to do, but they didn't make any difference. I could pop a couple of the over-the-counter kind, and I would still lie there in bed and think about my husband. At first I didn't know the woman he was having the affair with—I hadn't met her—but I looked her up on Facebook after Jeff left me, so I knew what she looked like.

I would lie there at night and try not to picture the two of them together—my husband and this married woman from another town—but it was all I could think about. Or I'd start thinking about my son, who was right at the age where he really needed a dad to look up to and how unfair it was that suddenly my husband was setting exactly the wrong example for him.

Kelly is quiet again.

Jake might have struggled in his teen years anyway, but when his dad messed up like that, it really sent him crashing down. He quit going to youth group, he quit doing his homework, he basically just kind of checked out of anything that involved work or study or God or being responsible. He flaked out. I'm sure he wasn't doing drugs or anything like that, but I can tell you that he just wasn't himself.

Since Kelly has mentioned this in a public setting, we spend a few minutes on this topic, talking about her son's response to his father's misconduct. It's a topic worthy of a whole book: what happens to impressionable preteens or teens when their parents make ethical or moral mistakes that are highly visible and universally regarded as wrong? During our brief talk with the table group, several other moms report similar situations, preteen or teen sons who experience declines in behavior after their fathers break up the family or abandon the marriage.

After several minutes of conversation, we return to the topic at hand: an adult's physical health in the aftermath of divorce. For Kelly, the experience of being abandoned by her husband led to a loss of appetite, difficulty sleeping at night, and a much higher susceptibility to colds, flu, and similar types of illnesses and impairments.

Jeff walked out on us in November. Within a week or so after he left, I had a major cold, and it stuck with me forever. I wasn't completely well again until the following summer. It seemed I had a sore throat or a cough or other symptoms all winter long. I had all these cold and flu symptoms, and I couldn't ever get past them, no matter how many kinds of meds I tried. Even when the doctor put me on antibiotics for a while, I didn't get better. Maybe I should have had him put me on antidepressants instead of antibiotics.

Kelly laughs, but she is not too far from the truth.

Recent medical studies confirm that divorce may negatively impact the physical health of adults who experience it. Although much more remains to be learned, a variety of health risks and chronic impairments seem more likely in post-divorce adults, even if those adults eventually remarry.

We will discuss these health issues by looking at symptoms and markers and examining the underlying diseases or impairments that may be more likely in those who experience divorce.

SYMPTOMS AND MARKERS

Difficulty sleep or resting. Kelly's story leads off this chapter, because her situation is far from unique. After a divorce, many adults, both men and women, tend to sleep less, have more difficulty sleeping, and may lack enough rest for adequate balance and optimum physical health. This appears to be true across a wide range of ages and applies to both genders. It is a marker for those who leave the marriage as well as those who are left behind.

Anxiety plays a key role. Divorce is a stress-inducing situation for all concerned—particularly for a partner who did not initiate and perhaps did not foresee the dissolution of the relationship. Numerous studies confirm the positive impact of marriage on physical health, emotional satisfaction, and longevity, strongly implying that the absence of a significant relationship makes us less likely to be healthy, happy, and live long lives.

Restlessness, anxiety, and difficulty sleeping are reported by a high percentage of divorced adults who respond to surveys about physical health. Some of these adults resort to nonprescription medications such as sleep aids; a few consult a physician for stronger relief. Many neither self-medicate nor consult a professional, enduring long nights of tossing and turning, worrying and wondering, eventually drifting off into a light-sleep stage that does not refresh or renew them.

Temporary or continuing weight gain. In the months immediately following divorce, both men and women typically report weight gains ranging from ten percent to as much as thirty percent. Men who have been dining at home courtesy of a live-in chef and housekeeper are more likely to drive through a fast-food restaurant and load up on empty calories. Women who previously monitored their consumption and watched their weight may now relax their standards, consciously or unconsciously, resulting in weight gain.

Once again, anxiety is a factor. There's a good reason that so-called "comfort food" has earned its label. Eating a high-fat, high-carbohydrate food or meal can induce feelings of relaxation and comfort—while adding inches to our profiles and pounds to our weight. Both men and women appear to gravitate to comfort food as a response to stressful situations, and the end of a marriage is one of the highest stressors someone can encounter.

Eventually, particularly as a man or woman begins to consider dating again, some of this newly added weight may be lost again due to a deliberate exercise program or better dietary choices. However, it is not uncommon for a post-divorce adult to gain—and then keep—ten percent more pounds than he or she previously carried. In persons whose weight is higher than optimal, every additional pound produces additional physical stress for the body's various systems and processes.

If you have experienced a divorce and also gained weight, consider yourself normal. Also consider getting into a program that will reverse the gain now, regardless of whether you choose ever to date or remarry. The health you gain may be your own; the life you improve may sustain and nurture your children and your grandchildren.

Headaches and other pains. Robert, a reasonably healthy thirty-five-year-old male whose wife left him for another relationship, began having chronic headaches a few weeks after his wife departed. He had never experienced headaches before; this was new territory for him. Somewhat typically for a male,

Robert avoided professional medical advice, choosing instead to treat himself with over-the-counter drugs and remedies.

"I was taking extra-strength medicines, and they weren't helping," Robert told us. "I experimented with different brands and different doses and even different times of day. Nothing worked. I began to wonder if my headache was psychosomatic."

Robert's headaches were real. They became severe enough that he eventually consulted a doctor. After a specific regimen of prescription pain meds, Robert eventually got relief from the symptoms, although he continued to have headaches for nearly three years after his wife left him. Then, just as suddenly as the headaches began, they ended.

Neither Robert nor the doctor had any explanation for why the headaches had happened or why they just quit. Robert is not a medical doctor but believes that the stress of his wife's leaving led to his headaches.

Divorced adults frequently report more back pain, chronic or recurring migraines or headaches, and a variety of other aches and pains. It is entirely possible that some or all of these symptoms were present while the marriage functioned, yet they were masked somewhat by an overall satisfaction level within the relationship. After the end of the relationship, anxiety and stress tend to amplify and exacerbate preexisting conditions, with the result that a divorced adult may notice headaches more or experience back pain as being more severe.

As with all medical conditions, it is wise to consult a professional. This is especially true if you are over forty, carrying a few extra pounds, or already battling a known health condition such as high blood pressure or hypertension. Divorce can ramp up these conditions at a high rate, for reasons that are not fully understood. Rather than standing in the aisle of the pharmacy trying to become a doctor or nurse, you are wise to consult someone who has studied, graduated, and become licensed in the field of improving your physical health.

Trust the professionals. Tell them what you are experiencing, and be willing to listen to their advice and accept their prescriptions. You may not need prescription medications over the long term, but timely, appropriate short-term assistance may save your life—literally. The time for a check-up is right now.

More frequent colds and flu. Not surprisingly, under-rested and highly-stressed divorced adults are more susceptible to colds, flu, and other maladies typically associated with the winter season. A woman who may once have shrugged off germs and viruses may now feel as if she is attracting and welcoming them. They settle in and then somehow never depart. A man who prides himself on not missing work due to physical illness may find himself calling in sick and describing himself as "under the weather" for the first time in his life.

Divorce is like that. Once again, the anxiety and stress that may follow a divorce can tend to amplify preexisting or normally occurring symptoms. That cold you might have ignored now seems troublesome and very much a burden. The flu symptoms you have medicated with over-the-counter drugs may now cause you to retreat to the comfort of home and couch.

Although Robert worried that his headaches might be rooted in psychological issues, the physical results were nonetheless real. Robert did not imagine himself to have a headache: he actually had one. The sniffles and sneezes and scratchy throat of a cold or flu may linger in a divorced adult for weeks or months longer than they would ordinarily. The symptoms of cold or flu may be more severe or more intense with the result that you feel tired, miserable, and less motivated to carry out your usual duties, activities, and responsibilities. And if you think you're really sick, it's quite possible that you're right about that.

Increased risk of serious and chronic conditions. Research is exploring the possibility that following the emotional damage of a divorce, adults may be statistically more likely to be diagnosed with a chronic and ongoing health challenge such as diabetes or high blood pressure. There are also suggestions that such adults may be at a statistically higher risk for developing life-threatening conditions such as heart disease and cancer.

This is not a textbook for medical students; we do not presume to give you medical advice here. Instead, we report to you about current findings as doctors, counselors, and others study the aftermath of divorce and its implications for physical life and health. These studies are expanding daily; new learning is here and on the way.

No one is yet saying that divorce causes disease or that the end of a marriage results in a traumatic illness. Instead of a cause-and-effect mind-set, researchers are pursuing a situation-and-outcome approach, trying to discover what happens to adults physically and physiologically when they endure a traumatic experience in wartime or the loss of a meaningful relationship.

Here is what is beginning to emerge from these types of research: in the aftermath of severe trauma and emotional distress, humans are more susceptible to illness and disease, including conditions that pose serious health risks or life-threatening health challenges.

No one is claiming that divorce causes cancer or that relational trauma rewires your body into a diabetic condition. What is emerging from the research is that there is a statistically greater chance of an adult developing these types of conditions if that adult has been previously divorced. Research is drilling down deeper to explore and explain the reasons. Without yet establishing any kind of causality, the implications are important for all adults, and especially important for those who suffer the loss of a marriage and life partner.

Experiencing a divorce may impact your health at a cellular or genetic level, the level at which chronic disease starts and spreads. The present studies are looking at emotional trauma in general, including the break-up of a relationship, which includes marriage and divorce but represents the end of relationships more broadly. A long-term dating couple who break apart or an engaged couple who call off the wedding may experience the same emotional responses and perhaps also a similar impairment of health.

For whatever reasons, evidence suggests that men and women who have endured a serious relationship trauma are more likely to experience chronic impairments and serious or even life-threatening illnesses and ailments. On the list of high-impact traumas, divorce or the end of a long relationship ranks very high. Losing a partner is one of the most traumatic events adults experience. Whether the loss is via death or divorce, it can impact one's physical health for years to come.

THE VALUE OF PROFESSIONAL ADVICE

We were explaining these findings to a group of women gathered for a divorce-recovery group at a large church, and we were talking about how vital it is to visit the doctor, get all the routine screenings, and take good care of oneself in the weeks and months after a relationship ends. As we began to talk about these issues, one woman raised her hand. Although we were reluctant to break the flow of the conversation, we smiled and gave her a chance to ask her question.

"Don't you understand," she says with evident frustration in her voice, "that when I lost my husband I also lost my health insurance coverage? Right now I can't afford to go see a doctor, and I'm not sure if my kids are covered or not. My ex has talked about keeping the kids on his health plan—the kids, not me— but at least that will be helpful for my children if it happens."

Around the table other heads are nodding in agreement. Others have faced these same legal, financial, and insurance difficulties after a marriage ends. Some are also cut off from former health plans and from prior availability of affordable health care options for themselves and their kids.

If you have access to health care through an insurance provider, the days and weeks after a divorce are a great time to use your benefits, including regular check-ups and regular screenings. If your coverage allows, consider getting a baseline physical against which your future health can be measured. Many plans have annual benefits for recurring events such as mammograms, reasoning that early detection can lead to early treatment, saving costs and saving lives.

If you do not currently have access to health insurance coverage, it's time for some creative thinking. Do you know a nurse or a midwife? Do you know someone who is constantly up-to-date on natural alternatives to drugs or medicines, someone who seems to study health issues and is always bringing you new ideas? Right now is a great time to reach out and connect with one of your friends or family members who works in the health care field or who studies human health.

Small-scale walk-in clinics are beginning to spring up in discount stores such as Wal-Mart and Target and in grocery stores and other retailers. These clinics often exist for the purpose of aiding persons without formal health coverage. Instead of the overhead created by an expensive hospital, these smaller, more accessible treatment centers keep their costs low and pass the savings on to you.

In larger cities, many health networks provide "free screening days" on a regular basis, sometimes three or four times a year. Tune in and listen up: there may be a "health day" or similar event coming to a community college campus or a neighborhood park near you. If you live in an area with a high concentration of retirees and senior citizens, there is a strong prospect that community health fairs and other such events are happening on a regular basis. Don't let your young age hold you back from accessing free health care! Any time a free screening or free clinic or free event is happening, attend it and gather helpful information that you would otherwise have to pay for. This is good for your financial as well as your physical health.

Following a divorce, you are at a higher risk for health issues, which means you need to care for yourself with a higher level of attention. The responsibility is yours; don't wait for others to suggest that you see a professional. If you have access to coverage and care, optimize your program for maximum health. If you don't have access to insurance-based benefits, then it's time to find creative ways to access as much knowledge and information as possible.

Although this book does not endorse Internet-based medical services, it's worth noting that a great deal of information is now available on major medical sites such as "WebMD" and others. You might be amazed how much detailed help can be accessed via a computer at home, at the library, or wherever you have access to the Internet. Click, read, and learn!

SELF-CARE FOR DIVORCED ADULTS

As it turns out, much of the advice your mom gave you while you were growing up turns out to be based on the truth. Some of the most basic and simple approaches to self-care are also among the most positive and helpful—for your sake and for the sake of any children or other family members who may be dependent on you in these difficult days. Taking care of yourself is good for you, and it's good for your children.

In the pages that follow, we'll look at some practical, immediately useful advice that will help you gain or regain physical health, helping you look and feel your best as you cope with the loss of a relationship. Regardless of whether you choose to begin dating again, you'll feel better about yourself. The benefits of good physical health accrue directly to you and to those who depend on you. Those who love you will celebrate with you as you build healthy habits and choose wisely.

Taking good care of yourself begins at home.

SIMPLE STRATEGIES FOR GETTING ENOUGH REST

"When my children were young, my husband and I developed this whole bedtime routine for them," Carrie tells us.

We would put the same things in motion every night at the same set times. There was a whole forty-five-minute process of what it meant to have bedtime.

The rituals were very good for our kids; we were firm, consistent, inflexible, and just stuck to the routine. So the kids adjusted, and it became a fun part of their day instead of something to fight against or dread. But what I noticed back then was that having a set bedtime for the kids was also great for my husband and me. We were able to have more time together, because we already knew what time the kids would be settled in for the night.

Carrie sighs and then describes a divorce in which her husband left her for an attractive woman who worked with her husband every day in a busy auto dealership. "She is really good-looking, and she knows how to use that to maximum effect," Carrie says with a wry smile. "I mean, my ex-husband is responsible too—it takes two people to have an affair—but I really believe she was after him from the start. I blame her more than I blame him."

After her marriage ended, Carrie had trouble sleeping. Her children were older, going to elementary school, and even after they were settled down for the night, Carrie was restless, anxious, and sleep-deprived.

I was actually praying about that one night. I hadn't been sleeping well, and it was very late, and I was praying about other things. Then it kind of hit me—why not ask God to help me sleep? As simple as that sounds, it hadn't occurred to me.

So I prayed and asked God to help me start sleeping better; then I remembered a CD that we always played for my kids at their bedtime as part of their rituals when they were younger. I hadn't thought of that CD for several years; we never listened to it except at bedtime when I played it in the kids' room as they settled in for their sleep.

Anyway, the CD is called *Golden Slumber*, and it's a whole album of contemporary lullabies in these great arrangements. It was magical for the kids; that CD was the last step of putting them down for the night: dim the light, cue the music, and they often were asleep by the second or third song

So I prayed and asked God to help me sleep, and the next thing I knew, I remembered that CD. I found it, started playing it, not for kids but for me in my own room when it was my own bedtime

Should I admit in your new book that having the same CD playing every night, this gentle CD of contemporary lullabies that was designed for kids to listen to, really works for me? I lie there in bed, and the music starts to soothe me and calm me down, and the next thing you know, I'm sleeping. I prefer to not take any meds; I just try to watch my caffeine, and then I play the CD every night, very quietly, in my own room.

It's working for me, and I'm sleeping well now. I think God is the one who reminded me of it, because I hadn't thought of it until I prayed.

Your strategies for getting enough rest might include any or all of the following helpful ideas: stress-reducing music, getting off the computer or away from the television as you begin preparing for bed, doing some light reading, taking a hot bath, or drinking a warm cup of milk, cocoa, or tea. We'll have more to say about tea in the section that follows.

One of the problems of modern life is that we are bombarded by visual images—television and computer screens—and many distractions that flood our minds with thoughts and ideas, even at a subconscious level. Pulling away from these distractions is enormously helpful, especially as the day winds down and it's time to get your health-giving rest.

As you prepare for restorative sleep, the key is to condition yourself to slow down, calm down, be less active and less agitated, and to think about things that are positive and encouraging. As you end your day, make an intentional choice to move away from anxiety and worry and reflect upon your blessings and gifts. Saturate your thoughts with uplifting ideas and encouraging themes such as God's promises to His children. As you begin to do this in a routine and recurring way, you will condition your mind and your body to enter into a restful and relaxing state as the day ends and the night begins. Over time, your body will acclimate to these patterns and will work for you and with you instead of against you. Your mind will quit racing as you lie down to sleep at night, and you will be focused instead on God's good gifts and the many benefits of walking in faith.

Drink plenty of liquids—and choose the right beverages. Staying properly hydrated at all times is essential to good health, but it is especially important for an adult who is under stress. The more stress you face, the more vital it is to drink plenty of liquids; and be sure you're choosing the kinds of liquids that actually hydrate and help.

Plain old water remains the beverage of choice. There's no need to rush out and buy designer water in a stylish bottle; grab a case of generic bottled water at the warehouse store, or save even more by drinking from the tap. If you insist on filtering, buy a container-based filtering system at Target or Wal-Mart, and filter your tap water while it's in your fridge.

Plenty of water is your best choice for good hydration. If you're planning to buy bottled water anyway, today's vitamin waters have added benefits that you can scan by reading the labels closely. Some promise more energy, while others add antioxidants and other health-giving ingredients. But if you're on a budget like most divorced adults—you can skip the pricey waters and just drink from your own tap. We'll talk about vitamins a bit later in this section.

Hot tea is another excellent beverage choice for all adults, especially for those enduring stress. There are a great variety of herbal teas available that contain no caffeine at all yet can help calm and soothe you after a tough day of looking for work or caring for young children.

One divorced woman we interviewed for this book sang the praises of the daily chamomile tea she drinks at bedtime. This woman's nightly ritual includes reading Psalms or Proverbs as she sips a warm cup of herbal chamomile tea.

"It really helps me sleep," she tells us. "I'm reading something wise and good, and I'm sipping something warm and cozy. For me, the combination is helpful, and it beats staying up late watching television, which is what I was doing before."

During the daytime, both coffee and tea have health benefits when used in moderation. In limited doses—a few cups a day—caffeine may actually improve your health. Study results are mixed on this question with some saying that it may boost metabolism and help a person maintain a healthful weight. There is a steady barrage of articles in medical journals asserting that coffee is helpful to one's health if not used in excess. No one has suggested that six or eight cups of coffee per day is beneficial.

Green tea has been used in Asian cultures for centuries for its wide range of proven health benefits. A growing body of evidence claims that the antioxidants in green tea, which is less processed than black tea, can help the body reduce or even reverse the damage caused by radiation and inflammation.

You already know what beverages to avoid: sugary, sweetened drinks—whether colas or beverages pretending to be juices. Recent studies suggest that diet colas, although definitely less health-impairing than regular colas, may be implicated in an increased risk of stroke. Many of the sugar substitutes used in diet drinks are also implicated in an increased risk for various types of cancer.

Fruit juices have a healthy reputation but contain more calories than you may realize. In terms of the impact they have on your body, fruit juices are a huge jolt of sugar, just like a cola would be. So the healthy glow surrounding fruit juices is a bit misplaced; the sugar rush from fruit juice impacts your body's production of insulin and supplies you with a large dose of unneeded calories. Fruit juice is once again a "moderation" issue. If you choose to drink fruit juices, drink smaller glasses, and supplement them with water or tea.

Proper hydration lets the body refresh and replenish various physical systems and muscles, moving you forward to better health. All the body's physical systems—digestive, circulatory, respiratory, and others—rely on good hydration and a healthy intake of water and other liquids.

Vitamins, minerals and supplements. Once again, this is not a medical book, and we do not presume to offer you medical advice. Instead, we report in these pages some of the findings that are currently being explained in medical journals and the mainstream press.

When your body is under stress, having access to vitamins such as C and E can help fight off colds or recover from cold symptoms more quickly. Many doctors self-medicate with very high doses of vitamin C, believing that helps prevent colds and fight off germs and diseases.

A quick trip to the local drugstore or discount store will reveal a wide range of choices and forms of vitamins C and E. Many people choose to get these two vitamins along with many others in a daily multivitamin. Whether brand name or generic, there are multivitamins targeted to men, women, older men, older women, men who do energetic physical workouts, women who do energetic physical workouts—you get the idea.

Multivitamins are a huge industry in our modern world, and the array of choices is expanding daily. Many qualified physicians continue to insist that the best way to obtain the right mix of vitamins is by eating a balanced diet. Yet these same doctors will often quickly add that many adults do not eat a balanced diet, so a daily multivitamin is a good substitute for what's missing. If cost is a factor for you, learn to read the labels. As you compare high-priced brand-name multivitamins, you'll often find the exact same formula—or one that is very similar—available as a generic product. Why not save the extra money and buy generic?

You might enjoy doing some broader reading on the question of nutrition and health. We'll briefly discuss some of the emerging research surrounding some minerals and supplements.

Omega-3: If you watch television or read the newspaper, you've probably already heard that including more Omega-3 fatty acids in your daily diet is recommended. Foods such as tuna and salmon are rich in Omega-3 fats, yet some people do not care to dine on seafood. Increasingly, fish oil supplements in tablets and capsules are being marketed to people who don't want to max out eating fish but still want the benefits of Omega-3 protection. Such supplements may have side effects such as fishy odors or fishy tastes, yet they are more easily accessed than going fishing or dining out at a seafood restaurant.

One thing you may not have heard: what matters is the balance of Omega-3 versus Omega-6 fats in your system. One of the problems of our modern fast-food diet is that we over-indulge in Omega-6 fats—think hot and crispy French fries—while not getting enough Omega-3 fats. The ideal remedy involves cutting back on unhelpful and unhealthful Omega-6 fats while increasing the intake of Omega-3s.

Trace minerals, such as magnesium and zinc, play key roles in the body's ability to process food, send nutrients throughout the system, and keep persons healthy for the demands of daily living. Some take these and other minerals in tablets or doses, while others rely on a multivitamin to supply these trace elements in the proper amounts. However you get them—a balanced diet, a specific tablet or pill, or the all-in-one capsule of a multivitamin—you'll want to include these key minerals in your diet for optimum physical health.

Get physical: We have already talked about getting a physical. In this section we are encouraging you to "get physical" by getting yourself moving and including exercise in your daily and weekly routine. If you are depressed or despondent, you may become less active and less inclined to get out and walk, run, or participate. Motivate yourself to get up off the sofa or out of the chair, bend and stretch, and begin incorporating more physical exercise into your routines.

Not ready to join a gym? Try walking more than usual. Park farther away from the door of the church, store, or school, and walk the extra distance in both directions. Have stairs in your house? Try climbing them several times a day for no purpose other than the exercise. Walking and climbing stairs won't involve spending money, buying exercise equipment for your home, or joining a fitness center or gym. They are completely free!

Living in an apartment or condo? You may already have a fitness center within your complex or neighborhood. You thought it was a great idea when you signed the lease, but you haven't been back since. Now is the time: Go to the fitness center or clubhouse and take a good look at the equipment. Pick one or two pieces of exercise equipment that seem the most approachable for you—the ones you might actually be able to use. Find a time of day when you can invest a few minutes to working up a sweat and getting in shape. If you were a typical suburban homeowner, you wouldn't be able to simply step out the door, walk a short distance, and have access to a well-equipped fitness center. Celebrate the blessings and benefits of apartment or condo living!

Do you have a large church nearby? Go online and look at the programs and ministries provided by that church. Many larger churches feature exercise nights and workout programs that are gender-specific, nonthreatening, and don't require church membership for participation.

For single females, what could be simpler than showing up at a church and doing a workout with other Christian women? Often the church-based programs have contemporary Christian music blaring away as women kick-box, run in place, or move through a simple workout. If you're not a member of the church, this is even less threatening; you don't actually know these people, and you won't see them on Sunday. You're just a Christian woman who wants to get into shape—on the cheap.

Finally, if you can afford it and have one nearby, go ahead and consider joining that club, fitness center, or gym. Among the benefits of these professional centers is that you have access to personalized guidance and assistance, a pro or trainer who can tailor an exercise program or daily workout to your specific age, health, and level of physical ability. You'll get guidance, feedback, and direction as you work on specific muscle groups or on specific goals such as achieving better balance or strengthening your core. Gyms and fitness centers are popular for a reason: they help you stay motivated, get healthy, and reach your goals!

Stay connected to real people, not just your online networks: Medical studies consistently demonstrate the health benefits of being in meaningful relationships with other people. You may have lost a spouse, but you may still have brothers or sisters, parents, children, close friends, coworkers and others who care about you. Right now is not the time to pull away from these others; it is specifically the time to invest in relationships rather than withdraw from them.

Focus on others, not just on yourself. Get involved in conversations in which you are the listener more than the speaker; the one hearing instead of the one always talking. Learn what challenges others are facing; as often as not, you'll go home counting your blessings instead of feeling sorry for yourself.

The healthy give-and-take of human relationships keeps us energized and reminds us that we are not alone. Below the conscious level, we thrive when we are connected to others—when we know that we matter to someone. At the conscious level, we gain by building relationships of trust and respect, mutual support, and mutual encouragement.

Although you may have avoided them in the past, consider joining a small group at church just for the conversation and the connection. Pick up a new sport or hobby, not because you care about it but as an excuse to be with other people. Avoid solo entertainments like going to the movies alone and staring at the screen while munching popcorn. Instead, get into a bowling league and discover the joys of rolling a heavy ball down a wooden alley while other people cheer for you.

Get into the flow of life and get meaningfully involved in sharing with, caring about, and praying for other people. If you're a suddenly single mom who now has kids to raise on her own, look around. You'll discover a world filled with women just like you who are facing the same challenges; some of them are doing better that you, and some of them are behind you. Learn from some, and share your wisdom with others.

If you're a divorced dad who has only occasional custody of your kids, once again look around you. Today's world is crowded with divorced dads who see their kids on weekends only—or perhaps even every other weekend. Sit down with these dads and learn their strategies for staying connected.

As we worked on our book *Moving Forward After Divorce,* we met a busy dad whose relationship with his kids has grown immensely since the divorce and since his kids moved to another house across town. Today, instead of living in the same house as his kids but never seeing them, this dad gets text messages from his children almost constantly. They text him from school (between classes) and while on the bus (before and after school) with questions about homework and life.

I've never felt so connected with my kids before. They don't even live with me. I see them every other weekend for two full days and nights, but the rest of the time they're with my ex. Somehow this technology of texting has bonded us together in ways I never would have believed.

My kids may not tell me everything now—and they probably never will—but they tell me a lot more than they did when we all lived together. And all I had to do was get them unlimited texting plans for their cell phones!

If you get into the flow of life, you will quickly learn that you are not alone. Celebrate that fact, and you will begin to realize that the same challenges and issues you face are being faced by many others every day. Get out there and meet men and women who have a lot in common with you because they also are moving forward after divorce, recovering from serious trauma, and adjusting to a new normal.

Being involved in meaningful relationships improves your physical health and often improves your outlook on life as well. Regardless of the benefits to you, do your best to be a blessing to others.

Questions for Your Personal Study and Reflection

1. How are you sleeping since your divorce? Do you get more and better rest, or less rest and less good-quality time asleep? What are you doing about it?

2. How often do you awaken in the morning feeling rested and refreshed, ready to start your day with energy and vitality? How long has it been (if ever) since you got up in the morning feeling that way?

3. Did you pay attention to the suggestions in this chapter about having a relaxing and calming nightly routine as bedtime approaches? Do you regard this kind of thinking as useful only as children—or can you appreciate how this same kind of strategy might be helpful for adults like you?

4. Do you find that you are more susceptible to colds and flu symptoms since your divorce? Do you have a harder time shaking off the symptoms or recovering from a virus?

5. As far as you can determine, is your immune system stronger or weaker since the divorce—or is there basically no change? What do you do to strengthen your immunity or keep yourself strong against germs and viruses?

6. Do you have a pattern and practice of getting regular physical exercise? What do you do in terms of a personal workout or personal fitness? Do you have access to exercise equipment, a gym or fitness center, or some other place (walking trails, nearby school athletic fields) where you can exercise?

7. Have you gained weight since your divorce, lost weight since your divorce, or has it stayed about the same? What changes have there been, if any, in your level of appetite or your interest in eating? What are you doing to be sure that you have a healthful pattern of diet and nutrition?

8. If you have children, are you making good choices in your diet so that they also will make good choices, or do you say one thing but do another? How often do your children watch you indulge in excess calories, junk food, fast food, or other choices that a nurse or doctor would tell you are unhealthful?

9. Do you have access to vitamins or supplements? Are you regularly using a daily multivitamin or daily dose of vitamin C? Why or why not?

10. When was your last physical check-up? Who is your doctor, and when did you last have an office visit with him or her? If you have access to health insurance coverage, are you getting your routine and regular exams as covered by your policy? If not, have you explored your options at free clinics, traveling exam stations, and other similar places? You may be surprised at how many options exist for the uninsured and underinsured in terms of screening, exams, and check-ups.

six

IS YOUR FAMILY PREPARED?

"All I wanted was a father figure for my two growing boys," Jackie tells us, describing her reasons for rushing into a disastrous second marriage. Less than a year after her divorce became final, Jackie began dating a tall, handsome man who was a career military officer. He was also recently divorced. The two had a lot in common, and there was an immediate and passionate emotional connection.

When her military boyfriend proposed marriage after only a few weeks of steady dating, Jackie was ready to consider it. "We had talked so much already by then," she remembers. "We had so much in common. Both of us felt as though we were older and wiser because of all we had learned in our failed marriages."

Although her friends told her she was moving too quickly, Jackie didn't listen.

I knew what I wanted. I wanted someone I could love and someone who could get control of my sons and give them adult male guidance. Richard's military background was perfect; I could see him walking in the door and being the kind of commanding, authoritative adult we needed so desperately in our home.

> I was struggling with two nearly teen sons—Jared was twelve and Jason was ten—and both of them started acting up when their father left. I hadn't been able to control them before, but my husband would step in and help out. My boys always listened to him, at least eventually. But with him gone, they were out of control—a lot.

Jackie made a decision that seemed wise to her at the time, but she now realizes it was a foolish and unhelpful mistake.

> I said yes way too fast. I know I acted like a crazy teenager in love, but that really wasn't the issue. Yes, he was handsome, and yes, we connected very intensely, but most of all I was going for the man in the uniform, the guy who would command respect from my sons. My boys had just lost their father, and all I could think about was finding someone to replace him—sooner rather than later. When Richard came along, everything seemed just perfect.

But not for long.

Richard's top-down, military-style authority was immediately rejected by Jackie's two sons, neither of whom had any experience with quick obedience to verbal commands that were sometimes shouted and at all times voiced clearly in a way that seemed like boot camp.

Jackie recalls,

> Even when Richard wasn't actually yelling, he had a pretty strong voice. His ordinary instructions to the boys were firm and crisp and clear. This was not Mister Tenderhearted. This was Mister I'm-in-charge-here-at-your-house. Richard knew only one way to relate to kids, and that was by being the typical military drill sergeant.

Jackie's sons were not impressed.

"You're not my dad!" is how Jason responded to an early command from his new stepfather. Jason refused to carry out even simple commands from Richard, instead preferring the punishment of the day.

I wouldn't let Richard hit them or spank them, which is what he wanted to do. My boys had never had physical punishment, and we weren't going to start that now. So Richard would take away their cell phones, try to put them in the time-out box, or ground them from going to soccer—things like that. Very quickly, both my boys decided they would rather be punished than let some new guy tell them what to do.

Jared, age twelve, acted up in ways more typical of sixteen-year-olds. He began taunting Richard, almost daring his step-dad to punish him. In one typically heated exchange, Jackie remembers her oldest son yelling back after Richard had given one of his typical orders.

"My mom should never have married you!" Jackie remembers Jared shouting at his stepfather, livid with rage. "You don't belong here. You're not a real part of this family! I don't like you, and I never will!"

It was not exactly the idyllic family life that Jackie had envisioned. Instead, her days with Richard descended into constant fighting with the boys, and behind the scenes—constant fighting between husband and wife about how to best deal with the boys. Richard desperately wanted to use corporal punishment.

He kept insisting that my sons wouldn't respect them until he beat it into them. Can you believe that? Can you believe a twenty-first-century male would actually have that attitude toward raising kids and providing discipline? I think

I fell out of love with Richard a whole lot faster than I fell into it. The more I listened to his ideas about how to get control of my sons, the less I loved him—or even liked him.

Jackie and Richard were married for a little less than eighteen months, but Richard lived in the home for less than a year. Eleven months after marrying for the second time, Jackie found herself once again home alone and raising two sons by herself. Richard was gone, and he wouldn't be coming back.

"We would have been better off if I had never married Richard," Jackie says today with the wisdom of hindsight. "I can see now that it was a huge mistake, but at the time it made so much sense to me. I was desperate—I knew I needed help, and I really thought I had found some."

Jackie's disappointment is a lesson for all divorced women but especially for those who long for an adult male to provide guidance and structure for young sons. Sometimes when we get what we want, it is the opposite of what we really need.

AFTER DIVORCE, YOU'RE STILL A FAMILY

If dating after divorce while you're still busy raising your kids is interesting to you, read the next chapter, which is a divorce roundtable. This topic came up again and again with our panel participants. Clearly, this may be the most important issue to consider as you think about dating and relationships.

How many children do you have, and how old are they? What will their lives be like if you explore or create a serious relationship or a new marriage?

As your future unfolds moment by moment, remember this: if you are a divorced adult who is raising children, you are still a family. Your family photo may look different these days, but you are still a family, which means you must consider all your choices and decisions in terms of how the family would be impacted. To put it another way, how much change—all at once—is good for your family?

TRUE LOVE WAITS

Mindy knew what to do, right from the start.

As she talks about those decisions today, a dozen years later, she still remembers the emotions, the attitudes, the prayers, and the passions of those first few weeks and months after her husband left her.

Left to raise two young daughters on her own, Mindy felt led by God to postpone dating and relationships for a while— at least until both her girls had finished high school.

"I'm not trying to preach to other people about this," Mindy tells us in a crowded coffee shop. "I'm just telling you my own story. Other people can make their own decisions and come to their own conclusions. But for me, I really felt that God was leading me to do this."

Mindy closed the door on even the possibility of a relationship. To her great surprise, she got constant pressure from well-meaning friends and family trying to set her up on dates. Even her parents, whom she assumed would be loyal to her original marriage, which had just ended, got involved in trying to find her a nice man to marry.

"Your kids need both a mother and a father in the home," Mindy recalls her mom advising her at the time. "Your dad and I are praying that God will send you just the right man who will be a great daddy to your little girls."

For Mindy, this was hard to hear. She had spent a lot of time praying about this decision, and she felt very clear about God's guidance. *Could I be wrong?* she wondered. *Why are so many close friends, my parents, my siblings, and my coworkers pushing me to date? Have I misunderstood God's plan or purpose?*

I ended up doing some serious prayer and fasting. I know we're not supposed to talk about that, but after so many people were so pushy about me dating again, I went back to God and asked Him for more clear guidance. I took some time away just to pray. I did some fasting; I'm not going to say how much or what I did. Let's just say this—I was totally serious.

I came out of the fast more convinced than ever that God was telling me to put off dating until my girls were mostly or entirely grown. Although I was open to changing my mind if God led me that way, what really happened was that He affirmed everything He had already told me.

After that, it was much easier to tell my friends, my mother, and everyone else who gave me advice that I had already heard from God—I had prayed about it very carefully, and I was not going to date now or anytime soon.

It took a while, but people finally realized I was serious, and they left me alone about it after that. Even my mom quit bugging me about men and dating and a father for my girls. I could tell what she was thinking, but she quit bringing it up, and she quit talking about it. I am so grateful for that!

Meanwhile, while her girls were growing up, Mindy devoted herself to being the best mother she could possibly be. Her ex-husband remarried, and her daughters occasionally spent time with their dad and his new family. As the years passed and her girls grew older, Mindy never doubted her decision.

For me, there was this great moment one Sunday night when my girls came home from being over at their dad's house. My oldest daughter, who was just coming into her teen years at the time, looked right at me and said "Mom, I'm so glad you didn't get remarried when Daddy left us!

I mean, I didn't think I needed affirmation for that, but when my own daughter said she was grateful that I hadn't put a new man in our house for her to adjust to and cope with, that was an amazing moment.

While my oldest daughter was saying that, my younger daughter, who rarely says anything at all, was nodding her head in agreement. So we sat down together, just us three girls, and I explained to them that I had prayed a lot about it and that I really believed God didn't want me to be dating or getting married.

After we finished our little discussion time, my oldest daughter looked at me and said, "That makes a lot of sense, Mom." It felt great to hear her say that.

Mindy looks at us to make sure we're paying attention to what follows.

I would have made the same choices, even if my girls had pushed me to date. But it was so helpful for my girls to say that. They were watching their dad's new family, his new wife, the children she brought from her prior marriage—they were watching all that happen, and they were really glad that their home didn't have all that drama in it.

That's when I knew my decision was from the Lord's wisdom. Today my oldest daughter is in college and the younger one in high school. I am just beginning to realize that I might want to date again in the future. I honestly have not struggled with this or worried about it for all these years. Now, as I watch my girls make their transition into adulthood, I'm starting to ask myself whether I want a life partner for the second half of my life.

I don't know the answer to that question yet. Maybe I do want a partner, maybe not. I think once my youngest is in college I'll do some serious praying about staying single or considering marriage.

Mindy, who is now in her forties, has waited until now to begin thinking about dating, romance, and a potential remarriage. Could you wait that long? *Should* you wait that long? In the next few sections of this chapter, we'll look at some of the key issues involved in making your decision.

STUDENTS, LIFE LESSONS, AND SOCIAL SCIENCES

If you happened to read the dedication of this book, you already know that it is dedicated to my students at Southern Nazarene University, past and present. They are adults who are completing undergraduate degrees after being away from school for a while or adults who are working toward graduate degrees in counseling, social services, or family studies.

They are wise, experienced, and ready to learn, and they are a delight to teach. Also, many of them are divorced. They come to the classroom with a history of family and relationships that often includes the end of a marriage, some experience with single parenting, and a lot of attention to the kinds of questions we are considering in this chapter.

Sometimes during the final session of a class, I'll allow my students to bring their own children into our classroom. Without putting the kids under the microscope, we nonetheless have the chance to get a child's perspective on life, learning, divorce, marriage, and many other topics—most of the courses I teach deal with family studies and family life.

Long ago, Art Linkletter hosted a television program titled *Kids Say the Darndest Things!* Linkletter was right, and my classroom has reflected Linkletter's wisdom.

Among the many things I value about my students is that they are not interested in learning what is merely academic. They are not interested in untested theories or high-sounding monologues. Their interest is much more practical: *What works? How can we make it work? Is there reason to have hope?*

While counseling, speaking, and writing about family life over the past two decades, I've also had the chance to learn from my students and from their experiences in marriage and family settings. It is not uncommon for a student who has been divorced to reveal that he or she is also a child of divorce. It is not unusual for a student who has been divorced to reveal that he or she never really liked his or her stepmom or stepdad.

In North America, divorce has been a widespread phenomenon for the past two generations, with extensions back into a third generation. Before that time, divorce certainly existed, but it did not broadly define the culture. Starting during the 1980s, divorce has come to seem typical. In a class filled with eighteen or twenty students, I usually have at least twelve students who are divorced and several who were both children of divorce and are now divorced.

I owe a great debt of gratitude to these students for what they have taught me—drawn from their own experiences and their own observations. They are wise and wonderful people. If I weren't employed and able to teach them, I don't know how

I would learn as much as I am privileged to learn on a regular basis.

Against that backdrop, let's look at how social science has changed in the past few decades and how learning about divorce has impacted the way counselors and ministers deal with the aftermath of a shattered marriage and a fractured family.

PREVIOUS MYTHOLOGIES

In the 1960s it was popular to speak about a *good divorce,* or in other words, a divorce that was done well, had little negative impact on the children, and left two congenial, well-behaved adults in its wake who were no longer spouses but who maintained civility and what might be called "cooperative friendship."

This entirely mythological construction endured into the 1970s and even into the 1980s until the sheer number of children of divorce began to overwhelm the system of categorizing any divorce as *good.* Social scientists and researchers who had previously claimed that divorce had little if any negative impact on children suddenly had a wealth of both anecdotal and quantifiable data available to them that shattered the previous beliefs.

Those previous beliefs of a "good divorce" were predicated on the idea that everyone should get along with each other, be nice to one another, dwell in peace, and go separate ways after the end of a marriage and breakup of a family. Even the youngest child who experiences divorce intuitively understands that something deep and meaningful is changing and that this change is occurring in the form of a loss. Grieving the loss caused by divorce not only occurs during childhood but often accompanies the child of divorce well into adult life and into advanced age. Over the course of several decades of family counseling, we have worked with numerous adults in their fifties and sixties and older who were children of divorce and were still being impacted by the pain of their parents' separation.

If this was simply our own experience based on years of specializing in counseling post-divorce families, our observations might be valid but not broadly useful. Instead, the things we have learned have also been learned in the culture at large by social scientists, researchers, marriage therapists and family counselors, rabbis, priests, pastors, and parish helpers.

Finally, the literature about divorce and its impact on children has begun to acknowledge what children of divorce already knew: divorce hurts, and the pain continues for years. Although children can and do adjust to changes in their families and transitions in the way family life is done, the pain of separation and loss can endure across decades of later life and subsequent relationships.

Among the authors reporting these findings are Judith Wallerstein and Sandra Blakeslee. Together with Julia Lewis of San Francisco State University, these authors and educators were involved in a twenty-five-year project, Children of Divorce, that went deep in looking at divorce and its aftermath.

If the topic of children and divorce interests you, consult the recommended reading list at the end of this book for specific references to several books by Wallerstein, Blakeslee, and Lewis. This book is not an academic text but is intended for real people in their daily lives, and what is important to know is that there is a mountain of evidence that suggests that divorce *does* impact children and that the impact carries forward for many years. Even when divorce is done as well as possible and the parents behave amicably after the split, there are lingering issues and ample patches of scar tissue in the lives of the children.

If you are a mother or father raising your kids after a divorce, you're hoping for the best possible outcome for your children, and you have reason to hope. Yet there is a profound difference between hoping and working for good outcomes and pretending there is really no lasting damage to children.

Thanks to the sheer prevalence of divorce in modern culture, there is now an undeniable body of evidence that suggests that divorce has lasting negative impacts.

HOW CHILDREN RESPOND AND WHAT YOU CAN DO ABOUT IT

As we consider divorce and dating from a family perspective, we'll look at several ways in which children typically respond to the presence or possible presence of a new adult in their lives. For a much fuller discussion of these issues, including some highly meaningful case studies, see Wallerstein and Blakeslee as mentioned previously. You might also enjoy and learn from one of our earlier books on the subject, *Moving Forward After Divorce* (Harvest House Publishers, 2006). Over the course of several years as we worked on that book, we interviewed dozens of divorced adults, many of whom were raising children. What we learned from that project fills several hundred pages with stories, examples, and insights. *Moving Forward After Divorce* has now gone to its third printing, and we continue to receive a constant stream of e-mail and other feedback from readers that affirm the timeliness and helpfulness of this book for divorced adults.

CLINGING TO THE DREAM: UNREALISTIC HOPES OF PARENTAL REUNION

Perhaps the most common experience shared by children in the months and years following their parents' divorce is the hope or dream that their parents will one day—perhaps soon—put their marriage back together and restore the family to its previous intact state. Younger children may cling to this hope with amazing resolution and fortitude. What is surprising is that older children, including adolescents and teens, have these same feelings and aspirations. Otherwise savvy and worldly youth can hold out hope against all reason that Mom and Dad will make up, end their legal and geographic separation, and set up the home as it was before.

Much is made of the marital stress and relational difficulty that often precede a divorce. In previous eras, the assumption was that children greatly preferred the peace and quiet of a divorce to the arguing and fighting of having two warring parents at home. The bulk of research now affirms otherwise: children long for their parents to be together, even if they have accurate and negative memories of their parents bickering, fighting, and failing to get along. Life as it was, warts and all, is what children often hope will return—life when the family was whole, both parents were in the home, and everything seemed normal, even if it was difficult.

While writing this book, we spoke with Emily, whose parents divorced when she was quite young. Emily is now a part-time student at a community college, and she also works as a waitress at an area restaurant. Emily grew up bouncing back and forth between her mother's townhouse and her father's apartment. She had a bedroom in both homes and kept clothing, music, photos, and other personal possessions in both places. Although the majority of her time was spent at her mother's, Emily grew up back and forth between two worlds.

Would it surprise you to learn that Emily, now in her early twenties, still holds out hope that her parents will one day reunite? Over lattes and mochas at a coffee bar near her campus, Emily confesses that she still wants her parents to get back together, even though she has very few actual memories of the days when her mom and dad were a married couple.

They're perfect for each other; they just don't realize it. Dad has had a whole series of girlfriends, but none of them has been like Mom. Mom has lived like a nun most of the time, but it doesn't really suit her. She's more social than she lets on, and she'd do better in a relationship than she does on her own. She teaches school all day and grades papers all night.

My mom needs a life! My dad needs a wise, wonderful partner. And both of them would have that in each other if they would just wake up! I can't understand how they've stayed apart all this time. They are perfect for each other—an ideal match—and everyone realizes it but them.

Emily has much more to say on this topic, all of it centering around her conclusion that her parents belong together and should get remarried and restore the family to its original condition. What seems ironic to the casual observer is that Emily, now in her twenties, would never again reside in such a household, even if it reunited. Emily is longing for something she missed—and is still missing—even though she cannot return to childhood, move back in with her parents, and be raised all over again in an intact marriage and undamaged family.

You don't need to be a family counselor or a marriage therapist to hear the idealized view of life and the naive perspective on marital togetherness that Emily voices as an adult. She is much more sanguine about her own relationships and her own prospects for marriage; here she displays a worldly wisdom that is beyond her years. Yet when the topic turns to her birth parents, Emily turns back the clock and longs wistfully for a childhood she never had.

Emily is not alone. In fact, she is somewhat prototypical of other children of divorce we have worked with who are in middle school, high school, college, and even well into later adult lives. Far beyond their childhood years, children of divorce may carry forward this kind of idealistic, unrealistic hope. They dream that their birth parents will one day resolve their differences, rediscover their romantic attraction to each other, remarry, and in so doing put things right. These dreams and hopes are sturdy and buoyant despite the ever-present reminders that the original family has been lost or changed.

What can you do as a parent? As much as possible, your children should feel comfortable expressing their hopes and dreams, even if these childish ideas are quite unrealistic. Instead of quickly squashing a dream that is likely to bounce back anyway, listen well and hear the heart of your child.

If you are asked some form of the question "Will you and Daddy ever get back together someday?" you are free to answer it honestly, but do so with wisdom. Even if you strongly doubt a reunion with your ex-partner, express your perspective with love and truth. You might say something like "I don't know, honey. Daddy seems to be interested in someone else right now, so I'm not sure if he and I will ever be together again in the same way that we used to be."

You don't need to lie or be deceiving, and you shouldn't try to encourage any of your children's false hopes. But neither should you destroy them. Let the dream breathe, hear it out, and try not to feel threatened by it. After you've expressed your own opinion about your future relationship with your ex-partner, be sure to get this important statement made: "What matters, Chelsea, is that no matter what happens to your daddy and me, both of us will always love you! Both of us will always help you and be here for you. That isn't going to change, no matter what happens."

The future is unpredictable anyway; what your children need is not an accurate prediction about the future but a steadying reminder that your love and your care will follow them all the days of their lives. This is how you build security and strength into the life of a child whose parents are divorced or divorcing.

SABOTAGING YOUR DATES: FENDING OFF UNWANTED SUITORS

Another common behavior exhibited by children of divorce is a tendency to scare off, ward off, or fight off potential romantic interests for one or both of their birth parents. If you're a divorced mom raising children, especially if you are raising boys who are at or nearing their adolescent years, don't be surprised if your son opposes the idea of you dating someone or actively tries to sabotage your new relationship.

Mark was fourteen when his mother began dating a man at church. Jenny, Mark's mother, had waited two years after the divorce was final before making any effort to get involved again. After two years of waiting, she felt she was ready to date.

When she met a kind, attractive, divorced man at a Saturday night worship time, Jenny was ready to be available.

Mark, however, was having none of it. As Jenny brought up the idea of possibly dating this man, Mark opposed the notion right from the start. He began attacking the character, behavior, appearance, and conduct of Jenny's potential date. When Mark was around the man, he would act up by being abrasive, condescending, or distant. No matter how kind the man was—and by Jenny's description the man stayed good-natured and cheerful despite Mark's bad behavior—the young teen continued to do everything in his power to attack, tear down, and scare off the new male adult in his life.

Such behavior is extremely common and is primarily motivated by the same types of dreams and hopes that we discussed in the previous section. Consciously or unconsciously, your children may be trying to save you for their other parent, which explains their inner compulsion to keep you from finding happiness with someone else. Even if their other parent is in a very steady or live-in relationship, or even if your ex-partner is now married to someone else, you may discover that your children are protective of you and not interested in letting you explore your options.

This behavior will sometimes look like jealousy; your kids may appear to want to keep you all to themselves. It is not uncommon for a young girl to fear that her mother will love her less or invest less attention in her if Mom begins to date someone or gets involved in a serious relationship.

Because of this tendency, many divorced adults work hard to hide their dating relationships from their children. With younger children, hiding a new relationship—at least during its early stages—may be wise and workable. With older children, particularly teens, this attempt will almost always backfire. If you hide your relationship from your teens and try to pretend you're not involved with someone when you actually are, you are training them to behave in the same way when they are dating.

Is this the example you really want to set?

Family counselors can cite numerous examples of children working to sabotage the romantic relationships of their parents. These same themes play out in literature and on television and in movies. If you haven't watched it recently, sit down and watch *The Parent Trap*. You'll get the idea that when a birth parent wants to explore a new romance, children are quick to oppose the idea. Children can be creative and resourceful as they oppose the idea of a single parent dating and as they undermine the person Mom or Dad is hoping to connect with. Never underestimate the cleverness or the strength of children.

As a parent, what you can do? As we discussed earlier in this section, if your children are quite young, you may be able to hide the existence or downplay the seriousness of your new relationship, at least for a while. With younger children, you can often simply include the new person in your life into activities you are doing with your children anyway—going to church, going to the grocery store or Wal-Mart.

Younger children will not automatically assume you are dating in these kinds of settings. Church is church, and the produce aisle is where you get fruit and vegetables. For younger children, this is a much different scenario than watching Mommy get dressed up in fancy clothes, spend a lot of time fixing her hair, and wondering out loud how she looks. When Mommy behaves in these ways, even very young children realize quickly that something is up.

But if Mom is simply going about her usual business in her usual way and another person tags along who is low-key and agreeable, often the new person can be worked into normal routines without raising any red flags for the children.

With older children or teens, the situation is much different. It would be wise to prepare your children as much as possible as you begin to explore the idea of seeing someone. Talk with your kids at a heart-to-heart level. Tell them that you love them very much but you are lonely and you miss having another adult around the house to share life with. Be honest about your feelings—not overly dramatic but as open and transparent as possible. This behavior lets your children come into your world and helps them understand how life feels from your perspective.

If you do it well—consistently and slowly—even the more resistant children may move from opposing the idea of you dating someone to actively getting interested or helping. This kind of turnaround happens when the kids are involved right from the start, when they are connected with your emotions and your ideas and your feelings.

Much of the opposition and attempts at sabotage that kids perpetrate grows out of the adult's desire to hide the relationship, deny the seriousness of it, or otherwise fool the kids. Kids are smarter than you may realize. Teens are far smarter than you think they are, at least in some ways. Your efforts to deceive, conceal, downplay, or deny are likely to blow up in your face and cause them to be oppositional instead of supportive.

With older children and teens, as you consider dating and the possibility of a new relationship, you should move as slowly as possible and as openly and transparently as possible. Keep the speed slow and the communication strong.

Isn't this exactly what you want from your kids when *they* begin dating? You want them to take things slowly, and you want them to tell you what's really going on in a relationship, stage by stage. Since this is the way you hope for them to behave, you are very wise to model exactly this kind of behavior when you are the one who is dating—or considering it. Show them how mature, responsible people conduct the process of beginning or developing a strong friendship or a romantic relationship.

Wise parents are communicative, honest, and slow. The result is a family who moves together in the same direction, slowly adapting to the possible presence of a new adult in the home—not as a "right now" or "tomorrow" idea but as something that, if it works out, might actually be okay.

DIVIDED LOYALTIES: CONFLICTING AND COMPETING

Another issue that emerges as divorced adults consider dating is a tendency for children to be confused about loyalty issues. If Dad divorces Mom, and then Dad remarries a new woman, children gain a second mommy whether they want one or not. Before you begin to resent the new wife in this scenario, stop a moment and realize that being a stepmom is without question the most difficult role in the entire universe of blended family relationships.

In general, children are hugely loyal to their biological mother and therefore unlikely to bond quickly with a new female, particularly if that female tries too hard to assume a maternal or motherly role. Children already have a mother; most are resistant to the idea of adding another one. A child's universe simply does not have space for the two-mom concept. There is only one mom, and she already exists!

Karen remembers her son's poignant question as his dad remarried someone Karen regarded as both younger and smarter than her. Karen's son was a frequent guest in his dad's home, and the son began to like and admire his stepmother. How could he not? The stepmother was glamorous and fashionable and youthful—everything Karen believed she was not.

One day, freshly back from his dad's house, Karen's son was chatting away about his new stepmom until he suddenly realized his mother's disappointment and disapproval. "Don't you like her, Mom?" he suddenly asked her. "Do you want me to not like her too? Because if that's what you want, I won't like her!"

Although he already liked his new stepmom, the child was fiercely loyal to his mother and was ready to abandon a new allegiance in order to defend and protect her.

The movie *Stepmom* depicts a similar situation, as ex-wife Susan Sarandon adjusts to the fact that her ex-husband is now dating Julia Roberts. Who wouldn't be threatened by that kind of reality? Sarandon's kids, sensing her growing discomfort with Dad's new partner and somehow realizing Mom's feelings of inferiority and inadequacy compared with Julia Roberts, quickly understand that they need to make some decisions about loyalty and allegiance. As they process their own feelings and consider their mom's situation, they finally ask Sarandon, "Do you want us to hate her, Mom?" It's a question they raise with sincerity and poignancy as the movie explores a post-divorce loyalty contest.

This is a fairly common scenario, one that plays out in homes and families around the world on a regular basis. With a new stepdad or new stepmom in the picture, children have to work out their loyalties and their allegiances in the midst of vague and uncertain new relationships and boundaries.

"If I love my new stepmom does that mean I'm being disloyal to my real mom?" one pre-teen girl asks her Sunday School class as they discuss this very important issue. "Am I going to hurt my mom's feelings if I actually like my dad's new wife? I need to know, because I'm starting to like her already!"

Around this girl, other members of her class quickly begin offering advice; many of them have already been in similar situations. The suburban church this girl attends is similar to most, and blended families are typical here. Welcome to the new world of Sunday School classes! Children of divorce make up a growing number of the kids sitting around in those chairs and sharing in those lively discussion groups each Sunday.

What should you do? Try to get past your own feelings of comparison and competition if your ex-partner is involved in a new relationship. Few men who leave their wives for another woman actually get an upgrade; ask any marriage therapist, family counselor, or minister. Although it does happen, rarely are the next partners younger, smarter, and more savvy than the ex-wife who is left behind. Most divorced guys do not end up marrying Julia Roberts!

Try to set aside, as much as possible, any feelings of comparison or contrast. Instead of worrying about how your kids feel about you, reassure them of how you feel about them: "I love you. I will always love you. I will always be here for you, no matter what happens between your dad and me." Keep sending your children the affirming reassurance and powerful security of a parent's love, and make sure that message gets through loud and clear.

Do your best to not undermine or sabotage the new partner, although he or she may be an easy target. Speaking badly about someone usually fails to cause him or her harm, but it often tends to make you seem petty or resentful. You don't want your children to see you as immature, small-minded, and threatened by others. Go ahead and give them full permission to like their new stepmom or stepdad or the person your ex-partner is dating. Give them your approval to like that person and bond and connect with that person and include him or her within their circle of friends. With or without your permission, that outcome is likely eventually, so instead of fighting it, lead the way by allowing and permitting it. Show your kids that you have learned how to treat people with respect in all situations.

What we don't mean: If a new adult involved with your ex-partner is a threat or a danger to your kids, the above advice does not apply. You have the right and the duty to defend your children whenever it is necessary. You do not have to allow your children to be endangered or harmed, and you do not need to train your kids to like or connect with someone whom you genuinely believe is a negative influence.

HOW TO KNOW WHEN YOUR FAMILY IS READY TO INCLUDE SOMEONE NEW

Brady, divorced from his wife but trying to be a good role model for his teenage daughter, decided not to date anyone and to remain single. Meanwhile, Brady's ex-wife had a steady string of boyfriends, live-ins, and love interests. Eventually Brady's ex-wife got legally married.

Although Brady was free to date, in his own opinion he was not necessarily ready.

"I didn't know how Meghan would feel about it," Brady tells us. "And before I got involved with anyone, I needed to have a heart-to-heart talk with my daughter so I could tell where she was coming from. The last thing I wanted to do was send her the message that I was abandoning her or that I loved someone else more than I loved her.

I'm not sure you can understand this, if you've never been a divorced dad, but after my wife left me, I loved my daughter more than I had ever loved anyone in the whole world. I'm sorry if that sounds out of balance to you or inappropriate somehow. I am just telling you the truth. Take it or leave it.

After Beth left me, I focused on loving my daughter and caring for my daughter and being the best dad I could possibly be. Somehow, as the years passed, I realized that I loved Meghan more than I had ever loved Beth. Does this make any sense to you at all? I am just telling you what I experienced.

When Beth finally remarried—and she had never been lonely, if you know what I mean—I felt I was free to consider dating and maybe marrying again. But just because I was free, it didn't make it the right thing to do. Or maybe it could be the right thing, but not the right time.

For me, what mattered the most was Meghan's perspective. How would she feel if I dated someone? How would she feel if I eventually ended up proposing to someone and remarrying? If doing that would threaten Meghan in any way, I was ready to stay single—at least until Meghan had a family of her own. At that point it wouldn't matter so much what Meghan thought or how Meghan felt. She'd have her own life.

Brady stops his narrative and looks around the office.

I needed to talk with Meghan before I took even one small step in the direction of dating.

One weekend while she was at my house I decided we would get away to the Smokies—Great Smoky Mountains National Park—and spend two days hiking in the mountains. I didn't say anything to Meghan, but I wanted to have these kinds of conversations outdoors, far away from other people, so that the two of us could have complete privacy and Meghan could say anything she wanted to say.

We had always been really close, and I didn't want anything or anyone to interfere with that closeness.

Brady and Meghan hiked and camped in the Smoky Mountains, spending nearly thirty-six hours together in a time that both now describe as hugely important for their relationship. Brady told his daughter the truth—he hadn't started to date anyone and hadn't even started considering anyone he might possibly date—and before he did any of those things he wanted his daughter's sincere, heartfelt advice and counsel. This caring divorced dad needed to hear from his daughter's true heart.

Thinking back to that weekend in a national park, Brady tells us that he was greatly surprised by two things. First of all, Meghan surprised her dad by being very open to his dating someone. "I think it would be really good for you, Dad. I see how lonely you are, and I think having someone to talk to and someone to share your life with would be really good for you. So if you need my blessing or something, you've got it."

The other surprising thing was that after Brady had been so open and so vulnerable with his daughter, she returned the favor.

Meghan started telling me all this stuff about her own dating experiences. Some of it I wasn't ready to hear. Some of the things she told me she had never told anyone else. She was really candid and really open. I don't know if it was the mountains or the privacy or the fact that the two of us spent so much time together that weekend, but Meghan got crazy-honest with me, and I was actually kind of unprepared for that.

Unprepared—but grateful. It was a huge change in our relationship as father and daughter. I kept a lid on it and didn't say or do anything too dramatic, and she just kept telling me a whole lot more. After that weekend, and for the rest of her teen life and college life, she would tell me pretty much anything that was going on. I can't tell you how much that meant to me. What if I hadn't asked Meghan's advice about my own situation? What if I had chickened out and never gone through with that weekend of hiking in the mountains?

Everything I value about my relationship with my daughter today—she's married and has kids, and I'm a grandpa now—everything I value about that kind of started with our hike together in the Smoky Mountains. Both of us bring that up all the time. It was a turning point for Meghan and me, in a good way.

With Meghan's permission and encouragement, Brady made the choice to be open to dating. He didn't pursue anyone; he just quit being closed to the idea. After only a few months of being open, Brady noticed that women were paying more attention to him. At times he returned the attention.

How did Brady's story work out?

The woman who is now my wife asked me out! She made the first move, and I just kind of went along with that. Obviously I already liked her, but I hadn't done anything about it yet. We kept seeing each other at church and even in a few other places, but I didn't do anything. So finally she asked me out, and I said yes. I guess the rest is history.

Brady and his second wife were married on a snowy winter day with Meghan escorting her father onto the platform, along with the minister, to await the grand entrance of the bride.

I walked her down the aisle for her wedding, and in a way, she sort of walked me down the aisle for mine. I mean, there wasn't really an aisle, but Meghan was my escort for that day. We didn't have groomsmen or bridesmaids. Gina, my wife, had one of her sons walk her down the aisle, and I asked Meghan to walk in and stand with me. So those two kids were our witnesses and also our only attendants. We had a small wedding, maybe thirty people total, and it was quick and quiet but very meaningful.

Brady leans back in his chair, seeming relaxed.

I'm really content in this marriage. I don't know if I'm more mature, or more flexible, or a little bit smarter—but I'm enjoying this marriage more than I enjoyed the first one. I don't take this for granted. I count my blessings every day, and even though my first marriage was kind of a wreck, I'm a grandfather!

All of this began because a divorced dad asked his teen daughter to share her thoughts and opinions before he considered dating—a wise father, a mature and unselfish daughter, and now a second marriage that is healthy and thriving, poised to go the distance and last a lifetime.

Snapshots of Family Counsel According to the Age of Your Children

1. If your children are already in college or adults when you consider dating after divorce, you would be wise to ask their opinions, but you don't necessarily need to be limited by their counsel or advice. They won't be living with you, so they won't be immediately and directly impacted by your choices. Include them in your process and listen carefully to their counsel, but the choice of pursuing a relationship is entirely your own.

2. If your children are quite young—early school years or before—it's wise to include the man or woman you're interested in to normal family settings with your kids. Don't call these events dates, and don't primp, preen, or act in a romantic way. Just include another adult in your shopping or church or a day at the park. Let the new adult become a natural and low-key part of your family times. From that beginning you can—if you choose—grow slowly into a more typical dating experience. Your kids will have time to adjust to being around another adult who is not their birth parent. You will have time to watch how the new adult relates to your children and cares for them.

3. If your children are adolescents or teens, take it slowly. You may be wise to avoid dating until your kids are out of these particular years. If you do decide to consider dating or pursue a relationship, move slowly and be as open and transparent as possible. This is not the season for sneaking around and trying to do something without their knowledge.

Your kids may be smarter than you realize. What you want to do in this season of their lives—if you choose to date—is model the kind of relationship and the type of communication that you hope they will follow in their own dating and relationship choices. Model carefully, because what they see may be what you get!

Questions for Your Personal Study and Reflection

1. How old were your children when your marriage ended? How old are they now? In general, would you say they are coping well with the challenges you face as a family, or are they struggling to survive?

2. How have you and your former partner explained your divorce to your children? Have you been open and available as your kids asked you a stream of follow-up questions? Did you have any success helping them understand the factors and reasons for your divorce?

3. Do you understand the strategic importance of speaking positively about your ex-partner when talking to your children? Do you understand that while you do not need to lie, now or ever, you do need to actively frame your discussions of your ex-partner with as much charity, kindness, and positive thought as possible?

4. If your ex-partner is dating, in a relationship, or has re-married, how have your children talked about your ex and this new relationship? How do they seem to be reacting and adjusting?

5. If there is someone new in your ex-partner's life, do your kids seem to like or dislike him or her? How freely do you feel your kids speak with you when talking about either your ex or his or her new partner?

6. Have you talked with your kids about the possibility that someday you might consider dating? If so, how did they react? Were they in favor or opposed?

7. Do you understand the wisdom of dealing with dating differently, depending on the ages of your children? What did you learn from the chart of counsel-by-age-groups that is included within this chapter? Does this help you better understand how to raise the topic depending on how old or young your kids are?

8. Have you experienced any acts of sabotage by your children as you dated or considered dating someone? If you are a woman raising a male who is now a teen or adolescent, how does he react to the idea of another man in your life or another man potentially living in your home with your family?

9. Among your close friends and family, whom can you talk to about the prospect of dating someone in the future? Whom would you trust to give you wise counsel without a lot of unwanted advice?

10. Among other perspectives in this chapter, you heard from adults who decided they simply would not date while they were raising their children. Did this viewpoint seem extreme to you, or did it seem wise? Would you ever consider excluding romantic and dating relationships until your children were grown to college age or beyond? Why or why not?

seven

DIVORCE ROUNDTABLE
A FREE-FLOWING CONVERSATION
WITH DIVORCED
MEN AND WOMEN

We announced the topic well in advance, and the evening's attendance is good; everyone who registered for the class is there.

The small group divorce recovery class is called "Moving Forward After Divorce." The class, which we present at larger churches across the country, usually runs one night per week for five or six weeks. We've taught this class for the past five years after launching it as a Saturday morning workshop at North Coast Church in Vista, California. North Coast is a vibrant, dynamic, growing congregation led by Larry Osborne. The director of the church's busy and highly effective counseling center, Becky Apana, invited us to create and lead the workshop.

Since that first Saturday morning we've been busy adjusting, modifying, updating, and changing the course as needed. What we've discovered is that the struggles of today's divorced adults are remarkably similar and that the issues and obstacles are the same wherever we go.

Tonight the group is laughing and joking as the latecomers find their places around a large table in the conference room. Everyone knows what the topic will be, and everyone has an opinion to offer. Before we even begin our discussion tonight, the opinions vary from Trisha, who says she will never get married again so doesn't see a reason to date, to John, who is looking for good woman right now. Between those two extremes are the others in the class—some of them open to dating, some of them dating already. Meanwhile, the topic of dating after divorce engages everyone's full attention, and there is laughter aplenty before the formal conversation begins.

We've brought three pages of notes, wanting to be sure we cover the key questions. What we haven't decided is where to begin. As we listen to the banter of the group, which is made up of people who have already been meeting with each other every week for a month, we suddenly realize what our opening question will be for this particular group on this specific night.

We're sure of our choice, so after a brief time of prayer, we launch into tonight's discussion and roundtable.

FIRST QUESTION: If you were going to date again— we're not recommending or endorsing it—what would you be looking for in your next life partner? What characteristics or personality traits would you be hoping to find in your next spouse?

There are nine women and four men around our table, plus the authors teaching the class. When we raise this first topic, almost every hand in the room shoots up. Apparently this is one of the easier questions to answer—or so it appears.

Dorothy, around fifty or so, is the first to speak:

A good job and a track record of getting and holding and keeping a job for a long period of time. My ex-husband went from one job to another to another, and in between he never really looked for work. I had to cut out ads for him or go online after we got a computer or ask my friends at work and my friends at church for leads or opportunities. My ex wouldn't take any initiative, and he never seemed to care about keeping a job. I think the longest he ever worked at one place was three years, and that was driving a school bus, not exactly a high-paying or professional job. But I was proud of him for doing it three years in a row. That was his longest stint at any job during our whole marriage.

Rick, who has served as our class clown during the course itself, sees an opportunity for making a comment.

"How old were the kids on his bus?" he wants to know.

"Middle school and high school," Dorothy replies.

"Well, anybody who can put up with middle school kids for three years in a row deserves a medal in my book!" Rick says with exaggerated seriousness. As often happens, a comment by Rick relaxes the class into smiles and laughter.

"I was proud of him," Dorothy says after a pause. "I mean, most of his jobs lasted a few weeks or a few months. That one was three whole years."

Sitting next to Dorothy is Emma, perhaps a few years younger. Emma is raising three children, two daughters and a son.

My answer is kind of the same as Dorothy's. It's almost the same issue. I would be looking for someone who manages money really well, a guy who knows the value of a dollar and knows how to plan. I don't want somebody with a flashy lifestyle or an expensive car or somebody who buys me expensive gifts to impress me. I want a guy who clips coupons and knows where to find the bargains. I want a guy who is really smart with his money.

Several women in the group are nodding as Emma is speaking.

I wasn't ever very good at that. I've had to learn all those things the hard way. Honestly, when I was married I never cared much about what things cost. I didn't look at the price tags. I didn't shop at the thrift stores. I didn't clip coupons or use coupons. In fact, I kind of looked down on people who did that. I thought it was a waste of time.

I was wrong about a lot of things. How did we ever survive before coupons? My family doesn't do anything now without a coupon. We don't go out for fast food, we don't go to the grocery store or Wal-Mart, we don't do anything at all without scouring all the possible coupons first.

Emma is warming up to her topic.

So I'm saying I don't want to start over. I don't want to go back to being stupid about money like I was before. And I don't want to have to train a husband about how to be smart with money either. I want a guy who already understands how life works and who is wise about saving his money.

With that, Emma is through voicing her opinions. Across the table, Rhonda is ready.

Those two are basically speaking for me. There are a lot of things I would hope for in a man, but right at the top of my list is responsibility: how he manages his money and his time. When I got divorced, I ended up with half our credit card debt and a big car loan, plus the mortgage payments on our house. My kids and I were under water from the very start, and it didn't get better for a long time.

We are finally starting to make some progress. I paid off the car, finally, and I have refinanced my house two times so the payments are lower, even though the house is still worth a lot less than I owe.

So Dorothy and Emma are speaking for me too. I'm looking for the same thing in a husband. Can he manage his time wisely? Can he manage his money wisely? Basically, is he smart about life? Or is he emotional and immature? Those are my questions, and money is a big part of that.

Three women have spoken, so we interrupt the group to ask for a man's opinion. What is a divorced male looking for if he decides to date again? But before we can solicit a male perspective, another woman wants to be heard from.

Joyce's tone is serious.

If you get serious about someone and you are really thinking about maybe getting married to him, you should pull a background check. You should get a credit check and a full background check, and you should find out just exactly who you're dealing with.

There is dead silence in the room for a minute; the group doesn't seem to know how to respond.

We ask Joyce for clarification. We remind her that we aren't talking about pre-nups yet in this discussion. "Are you saying that in a serious relationship, if marriage is being considered, the woman ought to pay $50, or whatever the going rate is, and get a credit report and a background check on the guy?" Joyce nods her head emphatically.

Absolutely. Obviously you don't need to do that if you're not serious about him. But if you're talking about getting married, and you're thinking about it, I am telling you right now: get the background check and get the credit check. Don't take his word for anything—not anything. Find out if he owes money and how much money he owes. Find out how he pays his bills. Find out if there are legal problems in his background.

Find out right now, before you marry him. Don't wait until after you're legally married to him to find out what you just got into.

On that note, we close the question from the female perspective and again ask for one of the men in the room to tell us what he's looking for in a potential future partner if he should choose to start dating again.

Rick is ready for the question; he's been patiently waiting his turn.

Looking around the room to be sure the women are paying attention, he nods his head at the two teachers.

For me, just the average super-model. You know, perfect hair, bright teeth, gorgeous figure, ultra skinny—nothing out of the ordinary, just your typical average super-model.

The women are groaning—exactly the response Rick is hoping for.

Sylvia throws a pen across the table in his direction.

"Spoken like a guy," Sylvia says, shaking her head in mock disgust. "You just heard what's wrong with the entire male population right there!"

Rick is laughing out loud.

"Okay," he begs. "Okay, I was *kidding* about that, all right?"

The women aren't letting him off that easily.

"Maybe *you* were kidding," Sylvia continues, "but that's exactly how a guy thinks, if you can call it thinking! All men want is someone who is great-looking; they don't care if she's empty or stupid and has nothing inside. They just care about the wrapper. That's all that matters!"

Women are laughing and agreeing with Sylvia's perspective.

"You tell 'em, honey!" urges Dorothy.

Rick lets the room quiet down before giving us his real answer.

Okay, you've had your fun. Now here's my real answer. You already know a lot about my ex-wife; I've talked about her before in this class. And I don't want to make her sound like a terrible person—she really isn't—but she was so negative all the time about absolutely everything. If I got an award or a promotion at work, she found a way to minimize it or make it sound trivial and unimportant. If I did something to help out around the house, instead of thanking me for it, she would turn it into a criticism, like "Why don't you do that more often?" instead of just thanking me.

No matter what I did or no matter how well I did it, all I ever got from her was complaining and criticizing. Also she had a very sarcastic and very dark sense of humor. It was funny when we were dating. She would tear down our waiter who was serving us, or the food or the restaurant, or the movie we had just seen. And it made me laugh

But when we were married, all of a sudden I was her main target! And her dark, cynical humor was always aimed at me and what I did or didn't do. I can tell you that after a few years of that, I wasn't laughing anymore. I forgot how to laugh, and all I wanted was to stay away from home.

Without realizing it, Rick has turned a corner and become more transparent about his own life and his own history.

I'm not saying I was a perfect husband. I wasn't. I made a lot of mistakes. I saw some of them at the time, and I see a lot more of them as I look back at things now.

I know I wasn't perfect. But come on. What guy doesn't need a little bit of encouragement sometimes? What guy doesn't like to have someone in his corner, cheering for him, even if it's not his best day?

Rick gets quiet again.

Anyway, what I meant to tell you as my real answer is this: if I ever get married again, I'm looking for someone who is cheerful and positive. I think I might even like somebody who's naive—in the best sense—not stupid, just someone who tends to see the best in other people, you know?

For eight and a half years I was married to someone who complained about everything and criticized everyone. When you walked away, she stuck a knife in your back, and she laughed while she did it.

I'm through with that, and I'm not going back to it ever again. If I ever get married again, I'm looking for someone who is positive and encouraging and cheerful and happy. I had fun with you talking about that super-model stuff, but I don't really care how she looks. I think any woman is beautiful with a smile on her face.

Rick the clown has almost become Rick the preacher. His tone is different; his content is different. The women around the table have noticed, and they're paying attention to him this time—much more than usual.

Things are quiet for a moment. Finally Dorothy decides to break the ice.

"Rick," Dorothy says in her best faux-sweet voice, "I believe that's the first intelligent thing you've said during this entire class!"

With that comment the whole group, Rick included, dissolves into friendly laughter and animated conversation. Clearly, this topic strikes a chord in our group of divorced adults.

We've heard one man's perspective, so before going further we ask if any other male is willing to risk sharing what he's looking for if he decided to start dating again. As is typical when you ask men a question, there's a long silence, and the few men in the room look at each other, preferring that someone else speak up and share his feelings.

Finally John, who is already on the record as actively searching for his next wife, decides to share from his personal checklist for wife number two.

Here's what I'm looking for. I'm looking for someone who isn't clingy. Let me explain what I mean by "clingy."

Some women, once you act interested in them, even a little bit, get all attached to you and start acting like you're already married, and I don't just mean sexually. I mean they are always hovering around you and giving you those looks and racing way ahead of things. They get sticky and gooey and clingy and, at least for me, that's a big turn-off.

So I want someone who is kind of relaxed and laid back about dating—someone who is not in a hurry, not too quick to get all close and touchy. I kind of wish we could just have a strong friendship for a while without having to worry about romantic stuff and just see if the friendship is strong enough to make a marriage, you know?

As John's voice trails off, he looks down at the table in front of him.

I'm not sure if any of you really understand what I'm saying. You already know I'm looking for a wife, but I'm not just ready to jump into something without getting to know the person. I would like to have a nice, easy friendship with a woman and just do things together without everything having to rush to a conclusion.

Then, if that's going well and the woman isn't getting all ahead of things, then maybe I would be the one to bring up the future and ask how she felt about maybe someday getting married—married to someone or married to me.

I would talk about it just like that—about marriage itself first of all and then later about marriage to *me*. I'm probably confusing every last one of you because I really want to get married, and all of you know it. But I don't want to get married to just anybody. I want to build a friendship, and if the friendship gets really good, I want to turn it into a marriage. Then the marriage—this kind of gets back to how I see marriage now that I've been divorced for a while—then the marriage ought to be an even better friendship.

Marriage, at least the kind of marriage I'm looking for, is about finding a lifelong friend, someone you can laugh with and have fun with and end up growing old with.

I wish I'd had that the first time—I really do. But at least now I know what I was missing, and I know what I'm looking for next time.

The room is unusually quiet. Finally Emma breaks the silence. "I think that's what all of us are hoping for," she says softly.

The group takes a cookie and restroom break, and we look through a half-dozen other topics to find our next question. By the time everyone ambles back to the table, coffee cups in hand, we know the direction we'll be going.

SECOND QUESTION: Let's say your divorce has just become final, and let's say you already know that the single life is not going to work for you, that you're intending to remarry at some point. If that's true—you just got divorced, you do plan to remarry someday—how long should you wait before being open to dating and relationships?

Rick is true to form. "At least five minutes," he says with a sheepish grin.

Everyone laughs, but no one volunteers a different answer.

We wait, knowing people are processing their thoughts on this topic.

Sylvia brings us our first actual response after glancing around the table to be sure people are ready to listen.

If you can do it, I think maybe three or four years is the right amount of time. My only question is, if you already know you're going to be dating and you're going to remarry, can you really be that patient and wait that long? Because I think you should, even if you know you're not going to stay single.

I just think it takes that long if you're serious about working on your own issues and if you're serious about healing and recovering from the end of your marriage. I think it takes three or four years for most people.

Dr. Frisbie has been telling us to focus on becoming our best selves, on rediscovering our relationship with God, on caring for our kids if we have kids. Can you really rush through all that in a few weeks or a few months?

I know Rick was kidding about the five minutes, but I also know people who seem to start dating immediately or even before the divorce is final. I have two friends who both started dating when they were separated, before the divorce process had even officially started.

They were off and running in new relationships, and they were still legally married to their husbands at the time. I was trying not to judge them for that, but to me it just looked stupid, if not sinful.

Joyce volunteers:

I have a friend who is doing that. She doesn't go to this church, and none of you know her, but that's her story exactly. Her husband hasn't even moved out of the house yet; they're staying together because neither one of them can afford to live separately. So they're in the same house, and they are still legally married, and the husband has been having an affair for a while.

My friend, who goes to church all the time and considers herself a good Christian, is very actively dating a man from her church. She is still married, and her husband is still living in the same house!

I know what you mean about trying not to judge people. Of all people, I don't want anybody judging me, so I try really hard not to judge others. But do you believe that? She's married, her husband hasn't even moved out, and she's dating a guy at church.

Joyce's comment quiets the room again; no one expresses a thought.

Finally Rick has had enough of the silence. "What's her phone number? She sounds like someone I'd love to meet!"

Laughter breaks the tension in the room, and once again we're glad to have a flamboyant, outgoing sanguine among the members of our small group. Sometimes laughter really is the best medicine.

After a discreet pause, we return to the topic, taking a survey around the table to see how long someone should wait after a divorce is final before considering a dating relationship or a romantic friendship.

The women quickly agree with one another, sharing Sylvia's perspective that waiting several years is probably wise. Among the women only Emma offers a varying idea. Emma suggests that if someone is mature and self-aware, maybe as little as eighteen months would be enough time to wait.

> It depends on the person. It depends on how mature he or she is and whether or not he or she saw the divorce coming. Sometimes people are ready for the divorce and they are ready for the next steps, because the marriage ended a long time before it formally ended, you know? Sometimes the marriage was over for a long time, and then finally the divorce happened.

> So in cases like that, maybe the person wouldn't need to wait so long, because in a sense he or she had been working on issues already while still married. Maybe it could be faster in a case like that.

No one argues with Emma, but the general consensus among the women seems to be in favor of several years of waiting before dating.

The men chime in next. John says,

I don't think you can answer that question. I think it will be different for every person, because every person is different. My dad got remarried about six months after he and my mom divorced, and he's still married to his second wife. She's been the best thing that ever happened to him—no offense to my mom. And they got together in only six months. So I don't think you can tell all people they have to wait three years or else things won't work out, because my dad found a new wife in six months, and it worked out great.

Rick has been biding his time—he's ready to pounce.

"Six months," Rick says with a wide grin. "Six months. I could work with that!"

The group's laughter convinces us that we are probably done with this topic; it's time to move on to another area of discussion.

THIRD QUESTION: If your daughter were getting divorced, what advice would you give her? What would you want her to know in those first few days and weeks after her marriage ended?

Rarely, perhaps for the first time tonight, a male is the first to break the silence. Robert, who has had little to say during tonight's open discussion, volunteers our first answer.

I *do* have a daughter who is divorced. I could see it coming for a long time. Honestly, when she got divorced I was happy for her. I never did like her husband, although I really *tried* to like him.

But he always seemed like a player to me. I think when you're a guy you can tell that more easily about another guy.

This guy was just too smooth, and he wouldn't look me straight in the eye.

Even on their wedding day it didn't seem like he was giving his whole heart to my daughter. I watched him flirting with two of her bridesmaids before the service started, and I remember thinking, *Hey, buddy—aren't you getting married today? What are you doing flirting with these two women?*

Anyway, they were married for a little over two years. It turns out that he was cheating on her pretty much the whole time. She finally caught him, and he told her he always had stuff going on the side, but that didn't mean he didn't love her—or something like that.

Sylvia interrupts from across the table.

I know the type. I know exactly what you're talking about. And why is it that we women always fall for it? We fall for the charm, the good lines, the good looks, and the whole time the guy is just flirting with us. He's not actually making us the center of his world.

Robert used the word "player," and that's the right word, I think. It's like some men never grow up, and they want to have it all—a wife and kids plus everything they liked about the single life too—flirting and playing around and just being stupid.

After a short pause Robert finishes his story.

Anyway, my daughter is divorced now. And since I was already divorced from her mother when my daughter got divorced, I didn't feel like I could really give her advice, you know? I mean, my marriage had ended too.

From their body language, it appears that everyone around the table is agreeing with Robert. They intuitively understand what he's telling them.

So when she got divorced, I just told her that I loved her and that I would try to be there for her, whatever she needed. She ended up moving in with me for a few months while she looked for a job and found a new place. Later, not right away, I told her I was glad she didn't have kids.

She looked at me and told me that she wanted kids the whole time, but her husband kept saying he wasn't ready. That part almost broke my heart.

But I was still glad they didn't have kids. I didn't have any advice for my daughter, but I tried to love her and I tried to help her. What else can you do?

Robert has just given us one of the better speeches of the night. Sometimes when our friends or our families are going through tough times, they don't need our advice or our answers. What they need is our love and our help, which is exactly what Robert offered to his daughter.

After some time has passed, we ask him about his relationship with his daughter today.

It's great. She's dating a really good guy, but they're taking it slow. He's divorced and has two little girls from his first marriage, and he's afraid of making a mistake again. So the two of them are going slowly with everything, and I think that's the right speed.

If he asked me today if he could marry Amanda, I'd tell him yes right away. He is so different from her ex! This guy looks me straight in the eye when he talks to me. He asks my advice about stuff. He tells me the truth. I trust him.

Robert looks around the room. "Wouldn't you want your daughter to marry a guy like that?" he asks, mostly rhetorically.

Every head in the room seems to be nodding yes in unison.

We return to the question: "If your daughter were getting divorced right now, what would you want her to know? What would you tell her? What advice would you give?"

This time it's a woman who speaks up quickly.

I think Robert did it exactly right. He just loved her and let her move in for a while and told her he would be there for her. I think that's perfect! I think if my daughter got a divorce—and she might, it's not going well—that's how I would try to be. But I'm afraid I might speak up too much or talk too much or just plain be a mom too much. I kind of do that.

Emma's voice trails off, and Sylvia finds her cue and makes a small speech.

I would want my daughter to know that divorce is not the end of the world. I would want her to know that yes, it hurts, and yes, you have tough days. Life is like that. But divorce is not the end—it's a beginning.

I think after divorce you're kind of cynical and you kind of quit believing in romance and marriage. You think it's all been a lie and it's all fake, and you maybe give up on the whole idea of romance and marriage and finding your soul mate. You quit believing all of that.

But before you know it, you start to figure out that having one bad experience doesn't have to ruin your entire life. I mean, what if people gave up on their jobs every time they had a bad day at work? What if they quit going to school every time they had a bad day in class?

All of us have bad days and tough times and challenges to work through. We may feel like quitting, but we don't quit. And if we don't quit and we hang in there, one day things start getting better.

If I were writing a divorce book, and believe me, *that* is never going to happen, I think I would call it *Don't Quit.*

Everyone comments on this topic, but most of them echo what Sylvia has said. In general, people want their daughters to know that they are loved and valued, and they would tell their daughter not to give up, that despite the pain and heartache of divorce, life can get better in the future.

As we've prepared for this evening, we've been saving a question to be the last topic of discussion. It's a wrap-up for seven weeks of class time together, and it's a fitting conclusion for this eighth week, an optional roundtable that we know we may use in our next book.

We've thought and prayed about tonight and this group, and we've already decided on the question that will end our session and conclude our class. In fact, we believe we've had some divine guidance in selecting tonight's topics and in choosing the final question of the evening.

We take our last break; a tray of brownies is suddenly popular, and Joyce makes the final batch of coffee, decaf this time. People settle into their chairs. For whatever reason, it seems fitting and appropriate to pray before this final question, even though we prayed at the start of this evening and we have opened every previous class session with a time of prayer.

For a few moments the room is silent. We ask God for His wisdom and guidance.

Then, taking a deep breath, we ask tonight's last question.

FOURTH AND FINAL QUESTION: Looking back at the person you were before your divorce, and then comparing your previous life to the person you are now, how would you describe the changes in you as a person since your divorce? How are you different? What have you learned? What are you doing differently? How have your values changed or your behaviors changed? What do you know now that you didn't know then?

It's clear that the members of the class are giving this their full attention. It's a serious issue, one less likely to be interrupted by humor or joking around.

We summarize the question in this way: **Who were you before the divorce, and who are you now? Tell us about the changes in your life and why those changes have happened.**

The entire group is silent for several minutes, reflecting. We have so much respect for each one of these people. We have treated them as peers and co-learners during the seven weeks of class, but somehow they have also become friends. These are people we would gladly do life with and connect with just to be together. Our common experiences in class have bonded all of us together more closely. We know each other a lot better now than we did just two months ago, before studying divorce recovery together.

Rick, who has made us laugh so often during our class times, leads off with the first response, and this time he's absolutely serious.

> I was a jerk during my marriage. I didn't know it at the time, but I was a very selfish guy. My life was about me— making myself happy, having what I wanted, running my household my way.

It was always about me, all the time. Can you believe I never saw that—that I never figured it out? I'm not sure my marriage would have worked out anyway—my wife went back to an old boyfriend after they hooked up on Facebook and started chatting every night for hours at a time. Maybe my marriage would have ended anyway.

If she were going to cheat on me, and if she were going to have this whole secret online life—looking for new thrills or old boyfriends—maybe there was nothing I could do that would have made a difference

All I know is that when I look back at my marriage now, I see this big, selfish jerk at the center of it. Not my wife—me. I don't know if I'm much smarter now or if I would do better now, but I'll tell you one thing: if I ever get married again, I'm going to do everything I can to be a lot less selfish. I'm going to try to make my wife happy instead of insisting that the whole family spend all their time making *me* happy.

Can I do that? Can I do that well? I don't really know. But maybe becoming aware of your own selfishness is a good first step—kind of like you can't change or you can't get better until you know who you really are.

I know I joke around a lot in this class, but deep inside I'm realizing that I'm a selfish, self-centered guy, and my selfishness hurt my wife and it hurt my kids and it hurt my marriage.

Maybe I would still be divorced anyway. I guess I'll never know the answer to that. But looking back, I see how selfish I was, how selfish I am.

I really hope, if God gives me another chance at this, that I can be the kind of husband who puts his wife and his children ahead of his own wants and wishes. I'm going to aim for that if I get the chance, and maybe you guys could pray for me, that if I ever get married again I can be more unselfish.

Rick is done speaking, and Emma leans across the table to make eye contact with him so he will listen to her.

"You're going to be a great husband next time," Emma tells Rick softly. "If there is a next time, you're going to do just fine."

Is that a small tear welling up in the corner of Rick's left eye? It looks like one, but we look away, not wanting to embarrass him.

He's a bright guy, and he's just told us the truth. We like him, and it's obvious the whole class likes him too.

Emma, perhaps emboldened by her quiet comments to Rick, is the next to speak up and offer her response.

I am so much closer to God now than I ever was in my whole life. When I was married, I thought I was this good Christian woman who was close to God, but that was nothing compared to the way I am now.

I went to church, I took my kids to church, I helped the children's pastor and his wife when they were doing big programs. Whatever I thought a good Christian should do, I was doing all of that. Maybe I didn't spend enough time praying or something, or maybe I didn't give enough money to the church, but when I looked around, I was sure I was a pretty-good Christian and a pretty-good person. Emma stops her narrative briefly.

I didn't know what really walking with God could be like. I thought Christianity was all about church and doing things for God and living the right kind of life—obeying all the rules.

I was doing all that, and my life seemed good to me, but I didn't really know God, and I didn't really have a relationship with Him—not like I do now.

Back then God was this absent father who was always watching me from somewhere up above and making sure I was being good.

So since He was watching, I tried to be good. I think I did okay most of the time. I did the right things. My kids were okay. But I didn't really know who God was, and I wasn't talking to Him about everything that was going on in my life, and I didn't feel close to Him like I do now.

Since the divorce, God and I are tight—that's what I would say if you're asking me this question. God and I are tight now. Not that I'm a perfect person; I am a long way from that. But I know God is here for me, and I'm trying to be here for God too. It works both ways, and I understand that now.

Do you have to get divorced to figure that out? I hope not. But in a strange way I'm almost glad I got divorced. I have a real relationship with a real God. I'm not pretending anymore; I'm not just going through the motions anymore. God loves me, and it makes all the difference in the world.

As the group nods their approval, Emma realizes she has spoken wisely. She leans back in her chair, smiles at everyone gathered around the table, and is done speaking.

This evening Sylvia is the last to speak, and her comments are well worth passing along. She gathers her thoughts before speaking.

I don't want to sound full of myself. I don't want to sound like I'm some great person now; I'm really not. But what I will try to say tonight is that I am greatly changed from the woman I used to be when I was still married, back when my life looked great on the outside, but my heart was empty on the inside, and I had so much pain in my marriage.

For me, the biggest change is that I have learned who my true friends are. I have learned who really cares about me, and I have learned how to care for them and give to them and be generous with them instead of just caring about me all the time.

When my divorce happened—and my marriage had been rough for a long time leading up to that—some people kind of abandoned me, and most people acted as if they didn't know what to do with me. I felt like people, and especially people at this church, kind of avoided me after the divorce. I felt shunned; it seemed like people were literally going out of their way to avoid me.

That was the worst feeling in the world. I think that hurt me worse than the divorce. By then I already knew that my husband didn't love me; I had known that for a long time. But I really thought the people at church were my friends, and I thought my family loved me too.

All of a sudden I was alone, and everything was different. Some people abandoned me, and lots of people avoided me. So there I was. I remember thinking *Now what do I do? Do I have go to out and make brand-new friends?*

But there were a few people among my friends who really cared about me, and they showed that. There were a few people in my family—especially my youngest sister—who really supported me and stood by me.

I was standing at my kitchen sink one day, washing dishes by hand, and I was just crying. I am ashamed to tell you this, but after my divorce became final, even though my husband hadn't loved me in a long time and our marriage had been a great big lie for a long time, after the divorce became final, there were days I just stayed at the house and cried.

So there I was, standing at the sink washing dishes by hand and crying. All of a sudden I started thinking about those two or three people who were being so nice to me, and for the first time I really felt loved! I stood there and just thought about how much my youngest sister loved me. I thought about two of my friends, Sally and Susan, and how strong they were for me—right then. I was kind of overwhelmed by it, and I quit crying.

I remember standing there thinking that I needed to start being kind and generous to my sister and Susan and Sally. They were being so amazingly nice to me and my kids and generous with their time and their money. I didn't have much, but I knew I wanted to start giving back somehow.

That day at the sink was the start of a new me. It probably doesn't sound very religious or spiritual, because I wasn't at church. And it wasn't even God I was thinking about—it was other people. But for the first time in my entire adult life I felt really and truly loved. It wasn't a mirage. I wasn't imagining it—no one was pretending to love me. I was actually *loved* by a few people.

That changed me. That started me on the road to my own personal recovery from the divorce. I sat down with my kids, and we started plotting ways we could give back to my sister and give back to my two friends. Before you know it, my kids and I were laughing! We weren't thinking about our broken home or our fractured family; we were thinking about how to help someone else, how to thank someone else for helping us.

So I guess the thing is—I'm not a perfect person or anything, but I'm a lot more unselfish now than I used to be. I'm much more aware of who really loves me, and I try to love them back in ways that are creative and kind and generous.

I'm poor! You have no idea how poor I am. But I am a lot more unselfish than I used to be. I care about other people, I give to other people, and I help other people when I can. My kids do these things right along with me. And yes, if you want something spiritual about it, I'm a whole lot closer to God than I used to be. I think maybe I didn't really know before if God loves me. I had to find that out by other people loving me, really loving me, before I could accept or understand the fact that God loved me too. Does that make sense at all?

All of us are looking at her. All of us, in the deepest sense, are with her on her journey; we are very caught up in her narrative.

Eventually Rick speaks for us. He gets serious and shows his deeper side. "Yes, it makes sense, and it also points the way for the rest of us. What you are learning is what every one of us needs to learn in the midst of our own disasters. Instead of worrying about ourselves all the time, we need to wake up and realize that there are people who love us and that there is a God who loves us."

Rick is feeling eloquent.

We need to wake up and start living outside ourselves, beyond ourselves, giving to other people and serving them. That's what Jesus would do. Maybe when a divorce happens to us we forget about that for a while. But then Sylvia comes along and reminds us of what matters.

We need to be grateful to the God who loves us. And we need to be helpful and kind to the people who matter in our lives.

With that said, no one in the room feels the need to add anything else. Our class is complete, and our roundtable is complete, and we will go from here—laughing and saying our good-byes to each other—less focused on our own issues and more ready to serve and help the people around us.

If there is light for our journey, let us walk in it—and walk well.

RECOMMENDED READING

SELECTED BOOKS BY THE FRISBIES

Becoming Your Husband's Best Friend. Eugene, Oreg.: Harvest House Publishers, 2012.

Happily Remarried. Eugene, Oreg.: Harvest House Publishers, 2010.

Moving Forward After Divorce. Eugene, Oreg.: Harvest House Publishers, 2006.

Raising Great Kids on Your Own: A Guide and Companion for Every Single Parent. Eugene, Oreg.: Harvest House Publishers, 2008.

Right from the Start: A Premarital Guide for Couples. Kansas City: Beacon Hill Press of Kansas City, 2011.

SELECTED BOOKS BY OTHER AUTHORS

Croly, Jennifer. *Missing Being Mrs.: Surviving Divorce Without Losing Your Friends, Your Faith, Your Mind.* Grand Rapids: Monarch Books, 2004.

House, H. Wayne, ed. *Divorce and Remarriage: Four Christian Views.* Downers Grove, Ill.: InterVarsity Press, 1990

Shelley, Rubel. *Divorce and Remarriage: A Redemptive Theology.* Ablene, Tex.: Leafwood Publishers, 2007

Wallerstein, Judith, Sandra Blakeslee, and Julia M. Lewis. *The Unexpected Legacy of Divorce: A 25-year Landmark Study.* New York: Hyperion Press, 2000.

Wallerstein, Judith, and Sandra Blakeslee. *What About the Kids? Raising Your Children Before, During, and After Divorce.* New York: Hyperion Press, 2003.

ABOUT THE AUTHORS

DAVID AND LISA FRISBIE

Family counselors and best-selling authors David and Lisa Frisbie jointly serve as executive directors of The Center for Marriage & Family Studies in Del Mar, California. For more than two decades they have studied and specialized in the post-divorce family: divorced adults, single parents, remarried couples, blended families, and stepfamilies. Since the late 1980s they have been widely known as America's remarriage experts, because so much of their writing, both in books and in articles, deals with remarried life.

David and Lisa are the authors of seventeen books and dozens of articles about marriage, parenting, divorce recovery, and other topics in family studies. They have been interviewed and quoted in national media, including *USA Today*, *New York Times*, and many other venues. They have been guests on ABC-TV nationally and CBS-Radio nationally, as well as many local programs and stations across North America.

They have been on *MoneyLife* with Chuck Bentley and *HomeWord* with Jim Burns. Many of their books have been endorsed and recommended by Focus on the Family and other leading Christian ministries.

Their articles appear frequently in *ParentLife* and *BabyLife* magazines, and the Frisbies have been published in *Thriving Family, Holiness Today,* and many other journals.

David and Lisa serve the global Church of the Nazarene as Coordinators of Marriage and Family Ministries. In this role they are under the leadership and guidance of Larry Morris, Director of Adult Ministries for the denomination. Their area of responsibility is within Sunday School and Discipleship Ministries, which is led by Woodie Stevens. David and Lisa provide writing, editing, teleconferences, web copy, consulting, speaking, teaching, and training for a wide range of Nazarene settings and situations. They are frequently consulted by district superintendents and leaders of various district ministries. They enjoy being speakers and presenters at events including district Sunday School and Discipleship Ministries conventions and district ministers and spouses retreats—among many other venues. To date they have traveled to all fifty states, nine provinces and two territories of Canada, and more than forty nations to speak, teach, train leaders, or counsel couples and families.

David is an ordained Nazarene minister who has performed more than three hundred fifty weddings to date, both in the United States and overseas. In this capacity he has led pre-marriage counseling sessions for couples from many cultures and of many different nationalities. Both David and Lisa travel constantly; both are lifelong learners with a great appreciation for cross-cultural ministry. David Frisbie reports that he has performed a wedding in a twelfth-century stone chapel in Switzerland and on a remote island in the boundary waters between Canada and the United States, among other interesting and varied venues.

He is an adjunct faculty member at Southern Nazarene University in Bethany, Oklahoma, where he teaches courses in marriage and family studies for the graduate and professional studies program. David and Lisa have taught and lectured at colleges, universities, and seminaries worldwide, including teaching classes in pre-marriage counseling and pastoral counseling. David is a frequent speaker for chapel services and for baccalaureate and commencement sessions. He also speaks for "Dynamic Dads" events in public school settings.

Happily married since 1978, David and Lisa claim their life focus is helping marriages thrive and families become healthy. In addition to their special attention to remarriages and blended families, the Frisbies frequently minister to military couples and families. They also have a special heart for all who serve in ministry, doing retreats, conferences, and counseling for clergy couples, teen preachers' kids (PKs), and missionary families around the world. Their books have been translated into many world languages and are sold in a diverse array of countries and cultures globally.

To reserve a speaking event with the authors, contact—
Lisa Douglas, literary agent for the authors, at mountain-mediagroup@yahoo.com

Rachelle Gardner—rachelle@wordserveagency.com

For publicity, media events, and book-signings—
Laurie Tomlinson—laurie@keymgc.com

In addition to leading and teaching workshops and seminars about divorce recovery, single parenting, blended family life, and other topics, the authors lead "Teens of Divorce" workshops and retreats, at which teens from divorced homes can process their feelings and move forward toward healthy, positive relationships within their family circles. For more information about these and other types of events and ministries, contact Sunday School and Discipleship Ministries, Church of the Nazarene Global Ministry Center, 17001 Prairie Star Parkway, Lenexa, Kansas 66220.

"Let's make a special effort to stop communicating with each other, so we can have some conversation." —Mark Twain

In *Couple Conversation,* marriage and family therapist Ted Chaffee shows couples how to create a sensuous, smart, and deeply intimate relationship by building on the four dimensions of the human experience: body, mind, soul, and spirit. With informal explanations, an array of illustrations, and splashes of humor, Chaffee explores each dimension's purpose and helps couples discover new ways to use conversation to confidently develop intimacy in every aspect of their relationship.

Couple Conversation
The Art of Creating Intimacy
Theodore Chaffee
ISBN: 978-0-8341-2374-8

BEACON HILL PRESS
OF KANSAS CITY

www.beaconhillbooks.com
Available online or wherever books are sold.